Intermediate 2

Modern Studies

2005 Exam

2006 Exam

2007 Exam

2008 Exam

Leckie ✕ Leckie

First exam published in 2005.
Published by Leckie & Leckie Ltd, 3rd Floor, 4 Queen Street, Edinburgh EH2 1JE
tel: 0131 220 6831 fax: 0131 225 9987 enquiries@leckieandleckie.co.uk www.leckieandleckie.co.uk

ISBN 978-1-84372-666-1

A CIP Catalogue record for this book is available from the British Library.

Leckie & Leckie is a division of Huveaux plc.

Leckie & Leckie is grateful to the copyright holders, as credited at the back of the book, for permission to use their material.
Every effort has been made to trace the copyright holders and to obtain their permission for the use of copyright material.
Leckie & Leckie will gladly receive information enabling them to rectify any error or omission in subsequent editions.

[BLANK PAGE]

X064/201

NATIONAL
QUALIFICATIONS
2005

MONDAY, 30 MAY
9.00 AM – 11.00 AM

MODERN STUDIES
INTERMEDIATE 2

This Examination Paper consists of 3 Sections. Within each Section there is a choice of Study Themes. There is one question for each Study Theme.

Section A – Political Issues in the United Kingdom (answer one question)

Question 1	Study Theme 1	Local Government in Scotland	Pages	2 – 5
Question 2	Study Theme 2	Power and Influence in Decision Making	Pages	6 – 9

Section B – Social Issues in the United Kingdom (answer one question)

Question 3	Study Theme 3	Equality in Society: Gender and Race	Pages	11 – 13
Question 4	Study Theme 4	Equality in Society: Health and Wealth	Pages	15 – 17
Question 5	Study Theme 5	Crime and the Law in Society	Pages	19 – 21

Section C – International Issues (answer one question)

Question 6	Study Theme 6	Issues in Europe	Pages	23 – 25
Question 7	Study Theme 7	Issues in an Emerging Nation: Brazil	Pages	26 – 27
Question 8	Study Theme 8	Issues in an Emerging Nation: China	Pages	28 – 29
Question 9	Study Theme 9	Issues in an Emerging Nation: South Africa	Pages	30 – 31

Total Marks – 70

1   Read the questions carefully.

2   You must answer **one** question from **each** of Section A, Section B and Section C.

3   You must answer all parts of the questions you choose.

4   You should spend approximately 40 minutes on each Section.

5   If you cannot do a question or part of a question, move on and try again later.

6   Write your answers in the book provided. Indicate clearly, in the left hand margin, the question and section of question being answered. Do not write in the right hand margin.

SCOTTISH
QUALIFICATIONS
AUTHORITY

SECTION A – POLITICAL ISSUES IN THE UNITED KINGDOM

Answer **ONE** question only:

> Question 1 Study Theme 1 – Local Government in Scotland on pages 2–5
> **OR** Question 2 Study Theme 2 – Power and Influence in Decision Making on pages 6–9

STUDY THEME 1: LOCAL GOVERNMENT IN SCOTLAND

Question 1

(*a*)
Local councils spend large amounts of money on local services.

Describe, **in detail**, **two** ways in which local councils get the money required for spending on local services.

(4 marks)

(*b*)
Housing may be specially designed to meet the needs of elderly and disabled people.

Explain, **in detail**, the reasons why housing may be specially designed to meet the needs of elderly and disabled people.

(6 marks)

(*c*) Study Sources 1, 2 and 3 below and opposite, then answer the question which follows.

SOURCE 1

Article on Local Council Election Results

After all the votes in the local council elections had been counted, the overall result seemed to show there had been little change. Compared with the dramatic changes in the election to the Scottish Parliament held on the same day, the situation in the councils seemed to be largely the same as before the election. Across the 32 local councils in Scotland the overall result seemed to be little different from the election held in 1999.

However, in some council areas the political situation was altered. In Dundee City Council and Perth and Kinross Council, the SNP made gains, becoming the largest single party in each of these areas. They were unable to take control in these areas because their political opponents joined together to keep them out of power.

It was hoped that holding the election on the same day as the Scottish Parliamentary elections would increase turnout. However, in 2003, fewer than half the Scottish electorate chose to vote. In 1999, the turnout for the elections had been about 60%.

Question 1 (c) (continued)

SOURCE 2
Number of Councillors in all Scottish Local Councils

Party	1999	2003
Labour	551	508
SNP	204	182
Liberal Democrat	155	175
Conservative	108	123
Scottish Socialist Party	1	4
Independents	204	230
Others	2	0

SOURCE 3

Control of Scottish Local Councils after Elections in 1999 and 2003

Local Council	1999	2003	Change
Highland; Western Isles; Moray; Argyll and Bute; Orkney	Independent	Independent	No change
Angus	SNP	SNP	No change
Perth and Kinross; East Dunbartonshire; East Renfrewshire; Falkirk; Dumfries and Galloway; Scottish Borders; Fife; Dundee; Aberdeen; Aberdeenshire	NOC*	NOC*	No change
Stirling; West Dunbartonshire; Renfrewshire	NOC*	Labour	Labour Gain
East Ayrshire; North Ayrshire; Glasgow; North Lanarkshire; West Lothian; Midlothian; Edinburgh; East Lothian; South Lanarkshire; Shetland	Labour	Labour	No change
South Ayrshire	Labour	NOC*	Labour Loss
Inverclyde	NOC*	LibDem	LibDem Gain
Clackmannanshire	SNP	Labour	Labour Gain

*NOC = No Overall Control – no single party has a majority of council seats

The result of the local council elections in 2003 showed little change from 1999.

View of Shona Muir

Using Sources 1, 2 and 3 above and opposite, give **two** reasons to **support** and **two reasons** to **oppose** the view of Shona Muir.

Your answer must be based entirely on the Sources.

You must use information from each Source in your answer.

(8 marks)

Question 1 (continued)

(d)   Study Sources 1, 2 and 3 below and opposite, then answer the question which follows.

SOURCE 1

House Building in Scotland

Immediately after the Second World War, local councils, new town development corporations and the Scottish Special Housing Association undertook major programmes of house building. These continued until the mid-1960s. Slums were demolished and people moved to new towns and new housing estates in the suburbs. A high proportion of the available housing was in public ownership, with most people renting a home from the council. Increasingly, however, people wanted to own their own homes and by the 1990s private house builders provided most new housing.

In 1981, the government introduced laws that allowed tenants of public sector organisations to buy their home, often at substantial discounts. This led to increasing levels of owner-occupation in Scotland. In recent years, of the almost 20 000 new homes being built annually, over 90% were built by the private sector with the remainder being built by housing associations.

Since the 1980s, housing associations have become the major providers of new housing for social renting. They have also taken over stock transferred from local authorities and Scottish Homes. Housing associations also specialise in providing housing for particular client groups, such as the elderly or the disabled.

SOURCE 2

Housing Stock in Scotland by tenure*, 1981 – 1999 (thousands)

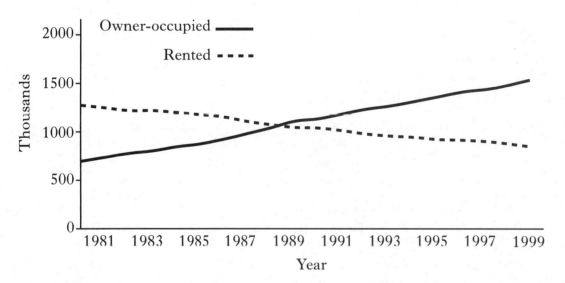

*Tenure – whether your house is rented or owner-occupied

Question 1 (d) (continued)

SOURCE 3

Housing Stock in Scotland – by Type and Age					
Date Built	Detached Houses	Semi-detached Houses	Terraced Houses	Tenements	Tower Block
Before 1945	38%	29%	19%	47%	1%
After 1945	62%	71%	81%	53%	99%
Total number of houses	367 000	450 000	500 000	487 000	56 000

Using Sources 1, 2 and 3 opposite and above, what **conclusions** can be drawn about housing in Scotland?

You should reach conclusions about at least **three** of the following:

* house building in Scotland

* changes in Scottish housing

* the tenure of Scottish housing stock

* the age of the Scottish housing stock.

You must use information from all the Sources. You should compare information within and between the Sources.

(8 marks)

NOW GO TO SECTION B ON PAGE 11

STUDY THEME 2: POWER AND INFLUENCE IN DECISION MAKING

Question 2

(a) | The Scottish Parliament has many powers. |

Describe, **in detail**, **two** powers of the Scottish Parliament.

(4 marks)

(b) | Pressure Groups use a variety of methods to try and achieve their aims. |

Explain, **in detail**, the reasons why Pressure Groups use a variety of methods to try to achieve their aims.

(6 marks)

(c) Study Sources 1, 2 and 3 below and opposite, then answer the question which follows.

SOURCE 1

**Number of MSPs elected to the Scottish Parliament by Party:
1999 and 2003 Elections**

Party	1999	2003
Labour	56	50
SNP	35	27
Conservative	18	18
Liberal Democrat	17	17
Greens	1	7
Scottish Socialist Party	1	6
Independents	1	4
Total	129	129

Question 2 (c) (continued)

SOURCE 2

Scottish Parliament elected for its Second Term

After the voting was over and discussions had taken place between parties, Scotland was governed once again by a Labour and Liberal Democrat coalition. This second four year term may be more difficult for the coalition since they have a reduced majority in the Scottish Parliament. The members of the Scottish Parliament are a more diverse group than during the first term. More parties are represented and more women were elected. However, the Parliament still has no ethnic minority member. The larger parties had mixed fortunes: some lost seats, others made gains. The Conservatives won three constituency seats in 2003; they had not managed to win any constituency MSPs in 1999, having all their MSPs elected on the regional vote.

Interest in voting for the Scottish Parliament has declined over the four years the Parliament has been in existence with turnout falling from 59% in 1999 to 49% in 2003.

SOURCE 3

Number of Female MSPs elected to the Scottish Parliament		
Party	**1999**	**2003**
Labour	28	28
SNP	15	9
Conservative	3	4
Scottish Socialist Party	0	4
Liberal Democrat	2	2
Greens	0	2
Independents	0	2
Total	48	51

The results of the election in 2003 for the Scottish Parliament showed little change compared with 1999.

View of Curtis Johns

Using Sources 1, 2 and 3 above and opposite, give **two** reasons to **support** and **two** reasons to **oppose** the view of Curtis Johns.

Your answer must be based entirely on the Sources.

You must use information from each Source in your answer.

(8 marks)

[Turn over

Question 2 (continued)

(*d*) Study Sources 1, 2 and 3 below and opposite then answer the question which follows.

SOURCE 1
Survey of Scottish Voters and Non-voters who were asked, "During the Scottish Parliament Election in 2003, did you . . ."

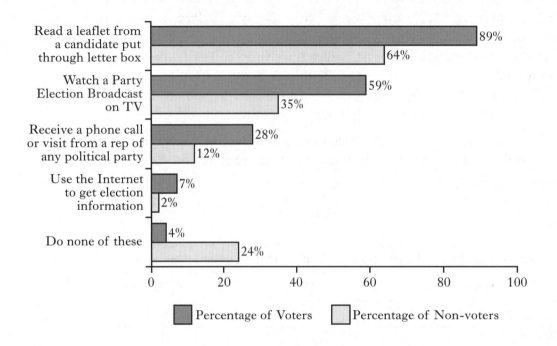

SOURCE 2

Percentage of People using Different Types of Media for Information in Elections in 2001 and 2003		
Type of Media	**UK General Election 2001**	**Scottish Parliament Election 2003**
Television	89%	56%
Newspapers	74%	60%
Radio	39%	34%
Party Election Broadcast	55%	49%
Internet	7%	5%

Question 2 (*d*) (continued)

SOURCE 3

Involvement in Politics

In recent years, more and more people have been taking part in political activity. Even although voter turnout in elections has declined and political party membership is at an all time low, political activity is still high.

It is not conventional activity linked to voting and joining mainstream political parties that is bringing people into politics. It is single issue campaigns, direct action and pressure group politics which are leading to higher levels of political activism. Often it is young people who are the most active in these single issue campaigns. Young people are the very group who seem to find conventional politics boring. The leaders of the main parties do not appeal to many young people, leading to especially low turnout in elections by young people. While older age groups still vote in large numbers, non-voters are likely to be young.

Suggestions have been made to increase the level of participation by young people in politics. Perhaps the political world can learn lessons from the world of television and show business. Millions of young people used the internet and mobile phones to vote in programmes such as Pop Idol and Big Brother. If politics allowed voters to express their preference by these methods, perhaps larger numbers of young people would use their right to vote. Many young people have strong ideas about how the world should be run, the political world must make sure that young people take the chance to express their views and ideas.

Using Sources 1, 2 and 3 opposite and above, what **conclusions** can be drawn about people's involvement in politics?

You should reach conclusions about at least **three** of the following:

• differences between voters and non-voters

• interest in politics

• use of the media

• young people and politics.

You must use information from all the Sources. You should compare information within and between the Sources.

(8 marks)

NOW GO TO SECTION B ON PAGE 11

[BLANK PAGE]

SECTION B – SOCIAL ISSUES IN THE UNITED KINGDOM

Answer **ONE** question only:

Question 3 Study Theme 3 – Equality in Society: Gender and Race on pages 11–13
OR Question 4 Study Theme 4 – Equality in Society: Health and Wealth on pages 15–17
OR Question 5 Study Theme 5 – Crime and the Law in Society on pages 19–21

STUDY THEME 3: EQUALITY IN SOCIETY: GENDER AND RACE

Question 3

(*a*) | Equal Opportunities legislation has benefited both women and ethnic minorities. |

Describe, **in detail**, ways in which equal opportunities legislation has benefited women **and/or** ethnic minorities.

(6 marks)

(*b*) | Gender or ethnic origin may affect a person's chances of participating in politics. |

Explain, **in detail**, the reasons why gender **and/or** ethnic origin may affect a person's chances of participating in politics.

(8 marks)

[Turn over

Question 3 (continued)

(c)   Study Sources 1, 2 and 3 below and opposite, then answer the question which follows.

You are an adviser to the government. You have been asked to recommend whether the Race Relations Act should be changed in order to allow positive action to increase the numbers of ethnic minority employees in the public sector.

Option 1	**Option 2**
Change the Race Relations Act to allow positive action.	Do not change the Race Relations Act.

SOURCE 1

Selected Facts and Viewpoints

- Ethnic minorities make up 1·6% of the population of Scotland.
- Ethnic minorities are under-represented in public sector employment.
- People of Indian and Chinese origin tend to experience relatively low unemployment rates.
- Concentrated efforts over the last 5 years have succeeded in increasing the number of non-white police officers by 71%.
- 63% of non-white males are in employment compared to 74% of white males.
- 32% of ethnic minority women are in employment compared to 68% of white women.
- More than half of ethnic minority workers in Scotland believe they were discriminated against the last time they applied for a job.
- Unemployment rates among minority groups are usually at least twice as high as those for white people, and highest for people of Bangladeshi, Pakistani and Black-African origin.
- In Scotland, 7·9% of teachers are from ethnic minority groups.
- Action is being taken in conjunction with the Scottish Executive to address the under-representation of ethnic minorities in the civil service, eg by encouraging ethnic minority graduates to consider careers in the civil service.

SOURCE 2
Police Officers from Ethnic Minority Groups in Scottish Forces (1998–2002)

Region	1998	1999	2000	2001	2002
Central	2	2	2	2	2
Dumfries & Galloway	0	0	1	1	1
Fife	2	2	3	4	3
Grampian	2	3	4	4	5
Lothian & Borders	6	6	11	18	21
Northern	1	1	1	3	2
Strathclyde	35	38	45	55	56
Tayside	3	3	3	4	4
Scotland Total	**51**	**55**	**70**	**91**	**94**
Total number of police officers in Scotland					**15 000**

Question 3 (*c*) (continued)

SOURCE 2 (continued)

Employment in the National Health Service in Scotland by Ethnic Group (1999)			
	Medical and dental staff, eg doctors and nurses	All other staff, eg administrative and cleaning staff	Total
White (%)	84·9%	99·4%	97·7%
Ethnic minority (%)	15·1%	0·6%	2·3%
Black (%)	1·3%	0·1%	
Indian (%)	6·8%	0·1%	
Pakistani/Bangladeshi (%)	1·4%	0·1%	
Chinese (%)	1·4%	0·1%	
Other ethnic minority (%)	4·1%	0·2%	
Total (number)	**9275**	**120 459**	**129 734**

SOURCE 3

Viewpoints

Positive action is the only way to redress the balance of years of discrimination and tackle the institutionalised racism in organisations such as the police force and other public services. If this is well planned and implemented then it is the only way that ethnic minorities in our community are going to make real progress. The NHS, police, local authorities and government departments should "lead the way" on race relations by ensuring more of their top jobs are filled by ethnic minority candidates.

View of David Morton

Positive action will only increase racial tensions and intolerance. Not only will it be resented by the white Scottish population, but also by those successful members of other ethnic minority communities who have worked hard to achieve the positions they deserve. Positive action would undermine their achievements. The UK Government and Scottish Executive are working through the New Deal and social inclusion programmes to improve employment prospects for ethnic minorities.

View of Raymond Morrison

You must decide which option to recommend to the government **either** to change the Race Relations Act to allow positive action **or** not to change the Race Relations Act.

Using Sources 1, 2 and 3 above and opposite, **which option would you choose**?

Give reasons to **support** your choice.

Explain why you did not make the other choice.

Your answer must be based on all the Sources.

(10 marks)

NOW GO TO SECTION C ON PAGE 23

[BLANK PAGE]

STUDY THEME 4: EQUALITY IN SOCIETY: HEALTH AND WEALTH

Question 4

(*a*) | Voluntary agencies and families help meet the health needs of the elderly and the income needs of lone parents in Scotland. |

Describe, **in detail**, ways in which the health needs of the elderly **and/or** the income needs of lone parents can be met by voluntary agencies and families.

(6 marks)

Answer either (*b*)(i) or (*b*)(ii)

(*b*) (i) | Private health care has advantages and disadvantages for both patients and the NHS. |

Explain, **in detail**, the **advantages** and **disadvantages** of private health care.

(8 marks)

or

(ii) | Increasing state benefits has advantages and disadvantages for people on low incomes and the government. |

Explain, **in detail**, the **advantages** and **disadvantages** of increasing state benefits.

(8 marks)

[Turn over

Question 4 (continued)

(c) Study Sources 1, 2 and 3 below and opposite, then answer the question which follows.

You are an adviser to the government. The government wishes to encourage lone parents back into work by giving them training through the New Deal for Lone Parents (NDLP). You have been asked to decide whether or not to continue with the NDLP.

Option 1	**Option 2**
Continue with the New Deal for Lone Parents (NDLP).	Do not continue with the New Deal for Lone Parents (NDLP).

SOURCE 1

Selected Facts and Viewpoints

The New Deal for Lone Parents (NDLP) was introduced by the UK Government in 1998 to encourage lone parents back into work by giving them training. There are 151 000 lone parents in Scotland, 93% of whom are women. The government set a target of 70% of lone parents in paid work by 2010.

- The majority of lone parents finding work with the NDLP are over 35 and with older children. Younger lone parents are less successful at finding work.

- 52% of lone parents in Scotland receive Income Support; they are either not in paid work or working less than 16 hours per week.

- The employment rate among lone parents in Scotland was 56% in 2002, an increase of 14% since the NDLP was introduced.

- The NDLP is voluntary and almost 70% of lone parents questioned in a survey felt that they would have found work anyway.

- 68% of lone parents have a high risk of unemployment compared to 10% of all adults. This is because they lack qualifications and skills.

- A quarter of lone parents on New Deal programmes would be no better off in work.

- Many lone parents have difficulty finding work, especially those with pre-school children.

- Around 10% of lone parents on New Deal programmes found the advice given ineffective.

SOURCE 2
Immediate Destination after leaving New Deal for Lone Parents (1998–2002)

Destination	Number	Percentage
Still on Income Support	10 830	41%
No longer claiming Income Support		
• In employment	14 770	56%
• On other benefits	280	1%
• Not eligible for Income Support	550	2%

Question 4 (*c*) (continued)

SOURCE 2 (continued)

Age of lone parents

Age group (years)	%
Under 25	10%
25–34	55%
35–44	28%

Percentage of lone parent families, by age of youngest child (2000)

0–3 years	30%
4–6 years	20%
7–9 years	18%
10–12 years	16%
13–15 years	16%

SOURCE 3

Viewpoints on NDLP

The New Deal for Lone Parents (NDLP) does not always benefit lone parents as it may encourage them into work which is low paid. This can result in a loss of benefits making them worse off. Children of lone parents may lose free school meal entitlement as well as clothing grants. The cost of travel to work adds to their expenses. Income from work may not be enough to cover childcare costs. The most important factor in being able to take a job is the availability of good quality, flexible and affordable childcare. Lone parents with high mortgages find the loss of housing benefit prevents them from being better off in employment.

View of Mary Miller

The New Deal for Lone Parents (NDLP) has benefited many lone parent families. Many lone parents lack qualifications and recent work experience which tends to prevent them from getting well-paid jobs. NDLP is based on one-to-one advice and guidance. A range of options for lone parents on the NDLP also includes help with training, self-employment and childcare support for lone parents working less than 16 hours per week. Those who had experienced long periods on benefits felt out of touch with workplace skills and lacked job references. The New Deal has helped to overcome employer prejudice against taking on lone parents. Training in new skills has helped to improve the self-confidence of many lone parents.

View of James Bashir

You must decide if the government should **either** continue with the New Deal for Lone Parents **or** not continue with the New Deal for Lone Parents.

Using Sources 1, 2 and 3 above and opposite, **which option would you choose**?

Give reasons to **support** your choice.

Explain why you did not make the other choice.

Your answer must be based on all the Sources.

(10 marks)

NOW GO TO SECTION C ON PAGE 23

[BLANK PAGE]

STUDY THEME 5: CRIME AND THE LAW IN SOCIETY

Question 5

(*a*) | Scotland has its own system of Courts.

Describe, **in detail**, the Scottish system of Courts.

(6 marks)

(*b*) | The legal age for buying alcohol is 18 years.

Explain, **in detail**, the **arguments for** and **against** increasing the legal age for buying alcohol.

(8 marks)

[Turn over

Question 5 (continued)

(c) Study Sources 1, 2 and 3 below and opposite, then answer the question which follows.

You are an adviser to the Scottish Executive. You have been asked to recommend whether or not the police should be given extra powers to disperse groups of young people from public places.

Option 1	**Option 2**
Give the police extra powers to disperse groups of young people from public places.	Do not give the police extra powers to disperse groups of young people from public places.

SOURCE 1

Selected Facts and Viewpoints

- In a System 3 poll almost 90% of the public agreed that the Scottish Executive, in tackling anti-social behaviour, should focus on young people.

- The number of police officers on the beat would have to increase if police were to be given more powers to move on groups of young people.

- Some people say anti-social behaviour by young people is a symptom of poverty.

- Young people would like to see more provision of "chill out" and "hang out" areas they can use.

- Police figures show that around half of public disorder incidents relate to "nuisance youths".

- One Scot in four does not feel safe walking in their neighbourhood alone at night.

- The largest increase in reported crimes was for those regarded as "less serious".

- 44% of young people interviewed believe they could make a difference to their local communities but are unlikely to be listened to.

- In a survey on anti-social behaviour caused by young people, 61% of those surveyed felt it was a big or fairly big problem; 12% thought it was not a problem at all.

SOURCE 2
Crime Rates in Scotland by Age of Population (1999)

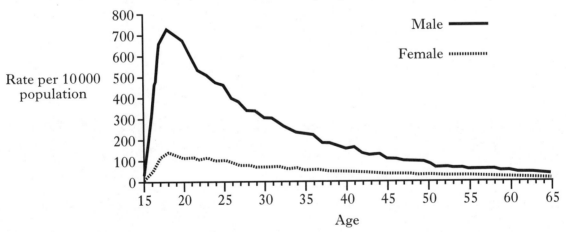

Rate per 10 000 population

Male ——
Female ·········

Age

"Best places to be" Survey 2003

Young people were asked "Where are the best places to be during the holidays?"	
Friend's home	51%
Hanging out in street away from adults	38%
Home	38%
Sports centre	20%
Youth club	10%

Question 5 (c) (continued)

SOURCE 2 (continued)
Survey of Types of Offence involving Young People

Offence	Percentage of those asked
Been involved in a fight with someone outside your family	19%
Travelled on a bus or train without paying or with an incorrect fare	15%
Deliberately damaged property	8%
Bought or accepted things you thought were stolen	5%
Taken something from a shop without paying	5%
Stolen money or something else from home	4%
Carried a knife or weapon with you	3%
Deliberately set fire to someone's property	1%
Stolen a car or ridden in a stolen car	1%

SOURCE 3

Viewpoints on increasing Police Powers

Police must be given more powers to move on groups of young people, especially from places where graffiti is a problem, where under-age drinking is taking place and from outside off-licences. Scotland's streets are unsafe. The criminal justice system needs to change. Local communities are worried about crowds of noisy, violent youths intimidating people. This type of anti-social behaviour must be dealt with so that decent law-abiding citizens can enjoy a full life in their communities and feel that they can walk the streets at night without being harassed.

Police spokesperson

Police powers to disperse young people are unnecessary. This would alienate young people and cause further problems in communities. It could ruin the good work which has already begun to build positive relationships between young people and the police. To introduce such powers would be a breach of human rights. There are other ways of dealing with anti-social behaviour. Young people should not be branded as criminals. Young people of all generations have got up to mischief; it is part of growing up. Politicians should not over-react. Tabloid headlines exaggerate the problems in local communities.

Social Worker

You must decide whether to advise the Scottish Executive to give the police extra powers to disperse groups of young people **or** not to give the police extra powers to disperse groups of young people.

Using Sources 1, 2 and 3 above and opposite, **which option would you choose**?

Give reasons to **support** your choice.

Explain why you did not make the other choice.

Your answer must be based on all the Sources.

(10 marks)

NOW GO TO SECTION C ON PAGE 23

[BLANK PAGE]

SECTION C – INTERNATIONAL ISSUES

Answer **ONE** question only:

Question 6   Study Theme 6 – Issues in Europe on pages 23–25

OR   Question 7   Study Theme 7 – Issues in an Emerging Nation: Brazil on pages 26–27

OR   Question 8   Study Theme 8 – Issues in an Emerging Nation: China on pages 28–29

OR   Question 9   Study Theme 9 – Issues in an Emerging Nation: South Africa

on pages 30–31

STUDY THEME 6:   ISSUES IN EUROPE

Question 6

(*a*)
> There are differences between the education system in Scotland and other European countries.

Choose **one** other European country, not in the UK.

Describe, **in detail**, differences between the education system in Scotland and another European country which you have studied.

(6 marks)

(*b*)
> NATO still has an important role in Europe.

Explain, **in detail**, the reasons why NATO still has an important role in Europe.

(6 marks)

[Turn over

Question 6 (continued)

(c)   Study Sources 1, 2 and 3 below and opposite, then answer the question which follows.

SOURCE 1
New members joining the European Union in 2004

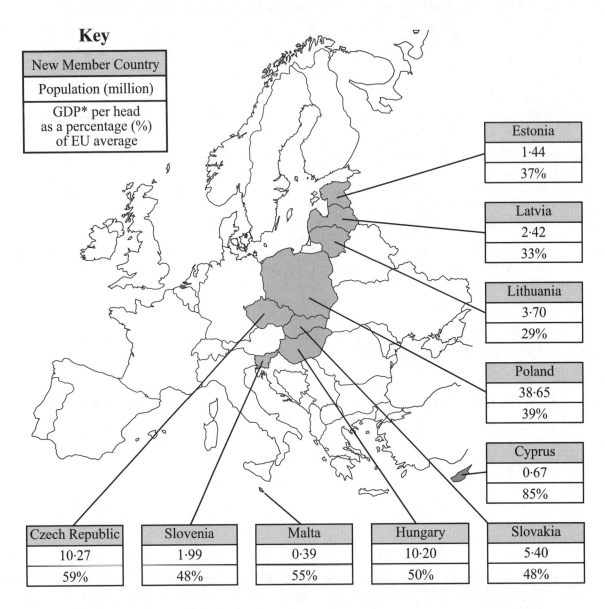

Key

New Member Country
Population (million)
GDP* per head as a percentage (%) of EU average

Estonia
1·44
37%

Latvia
2·42
33%

Lithuania
3·70
29%

Poland
38·65
39%

Cyprus
0·67
85%

Czech Republic	Slovenia	Malta	Hungary	Slovakia
10·27	1·99	0·39	10·20	5·40
59%	48%	55%	50%	48%

Population of new members: 75·13 million

Population of existing EU members: 376·46 million

*GDP (Gross Domestic Product) — The value of goods and services produced in a country in a year

Question 6 (c) (continued)

SOURCE 2

European Union (EU) money for the new members 2004 – 2006

The cost to the EU between 2004 and 2006 of the new members will be high and will increase over these years. But there will be a limit set on the amount of money the new members will get from the EU, so that the 15 existing members will not be faced with a huge bill in meeting the needs of these members. Most of the new members have a low level of GDP per head compared to the existing members. The existing 15 members will benefit from investment opportunities in the new member countries. There will also be an increased number of customers for goods produced by EU members. The EU already has a trade surplus with the new members because new members spend more buying goods from the EU than existing members spend buying goods from them.

Additional costs to the EU of the new members 2004 – 2006 (€ billions)

Category	2004	2005	2006
Common Agricultural Policy	1·9	3·7	4·1
Regional aid	6·1	6·9	8·8
Structural funds	3·5	4·8	6·0
Others	5·8	5·4	5·7
Total	**17·3**	**20·8**	**24·6**

SOURCE 3

Poland's membership of the EU

The membership of Poland will strengthen the EU. It has nearly 40 million people. It accounts for half of the total population of the new members. It will be one of the bigger members, like the UK, France, Germany and Italy. The people of Poland are very keen to join. In a referendum in June 2003 where the turnout was 59%, 77% of those who voted said they wanted to join the European Union.

The effects on the EU of new members

Businesses in some European Union countries could face competition from the new members. Wage costs are lower in most of the new countries than in the rest of the EU, so their prices may be cheaper. If businesses in the original member states do not adapt, they may find it difficult to sell their goods. If the result is job losses and rising unemployment, politicians may live to regret their decision to enlarge the EU. Migration is also an issue which could have a serious impact. Media reports claim there will be a large movement of workers into the existing member states.

The EU will benefit from the increase in the number of members in 2004.

Member of the European Parliament (MEP)

Using Sources 1, 2 and 3, explain why the MEP could be accused of being **selective in the use of facts**.

Your answer must be based entirely on the Sources above and opposite.

(8 marks)

NOW CHECK THAT YOU HAVE ANSWERED ONE QUESTION FROM EACH OF SECTIONS A, B AND C.

STUDY THEME 7: ISSUES IN AN EMERGING NATION: BRAZIL

Question 7

(*a*) | People in different parts of Brazil have different lifestyles.

Describe, **in detail**, the differences in the lifestyles between people in different parts of Brazil.

(6 marks)

(*b*) | Human rights issues continue to be a major concern for the government of Brazil.

Explain, **in detail**, the reasons why human rights issues continue to be a major concern for the government of Brazil.

(6 marks)

(*c*) Study Sources 1, 2 and 3 below and opposite, then answer the question which follows.

SOURCE 1
Comparative Economic Indicators, 2002
(Selected South and Central American Countries)

	Brazil	Argentina	Mexico
GDP*	$1340 billion	$391 billion	$900 billion
GDP (per person)	$7600	$10 200	$9000
Population below poverty line	22%	37%	40%
Inflation rate	8·3%	41%	6·4%
Unemployment rate	6·4%	21·5%	4%
Government income	$100·6 billion	$44 billion	$136 billion
Government spending	$91·6 billion	$48 billion	$140 billion
Exports	$59·4 billion	$25·3 billion	$158·4 billion
Imports	$46·2 billion	$9 billion	$168·4 billion
National debt	$222·4 billion	$155 billion	$150 billion

*GDP (Gross Domestic Product) – The value of goods and services produced in a country in a year

Question 7 (c) (continued)

SOURCE 2
Brazil's Trade with the USA ($ billion)

Year	Exports to USA	Imports from USA	Difference between imports and exports
1999	13·2	11·3	+ 1·9
2000	15·3	13·9	+ 1·4
2001	15·9	14·5	+ 1·4
2002	12·4	15·8	− 3·4

SOURCE 3

Brazil – Economic Progress

The new President of Brazil, Luiz Inacio Lula de Silva, known as Lula, became President in January 2003. He pledged to increase economic growth and to combat hunger and unemployment.

Some experts are not so sure he can deliver on his promises. One said, "In order to eliminate poverty we have to create wealth, and yet all the economic indicators show that Brazil's performance is poorer than other South and Central American countries." In 2003 there was a decline of Brazilian car sales which have dropped 22% in a year.

Davi Henrique, a Brazilian economist, is more optimistic about the future. He said "Give the man a chance. We know that Lula alone cannot do miracles but the signs are that Brazil is on the way to economic recovery." In August 2003, Brazil's overall trade surplus rose to $2·7 billion, which is 70% higher than in August 2002. Exports also rose in August 2003 to $6·4 billion, up from $5·7 billion in the same month of 2002.

Brazil still has serious issues to address. In São Paulo, the country's industrial heartland, unemployment is at a record high at 20% and 60% of people still live in poverty. Protesters recently criticised Brazil's Congress because of a new law that has raised the retirement age, cut public spending and allowed pensions to be taxed. Many protesters accused the President of breaking his election promises to the people. A spokesperson for the Government said the reforms were necessary to try to reduce Brazil's massive debt problem.

The Brazilian economy is strong and continues to improve.

View of a Brazilian Government Official

Using Sources 1, 2 and 3, explain why the Brazilian Government Official is being **selective in the use of facts**.

Your answer must be based entirely on the Sources above and opposite.

(8 marks)

NOW CHECK THAT YOU HAVE ANSWERED ONE QUESTION FROM EACH OF SECTIONS A, B AND C

STUDY THEME 8: ISSUES IN AN EMERGING NATION: CHINA

Question 8

(*a*)

People in different parts of China have different lifestyles.

Describe, **in detail**, the differences in lifestyles between people in different parts of China.

(6 marks)

(*b*)

The Chinese Government has been criticised for its human rights record in Tibet.

Explain, **in detail**, the reasons why the Chinese Government has been criticised for its human rights record in Tibet.

(6 marks)

(*c*)   Study Sources 1, 2 and 3 below and opposite, then answer the question which follows.

SOURCE 1

Timeline for the Severe Acute Respiratory Syndrome (SARS) outbreak in China

16 November 2002	The first known case of SARS was reported. The outbreak started in Guangdong.
11 February 2003	Chinese Ministry of Health reports 300 cases of an "acute respiratory syndrome"; with 5 deaths in Guangdong.
11 March 2003	Hong Kong officials report an outbreak of "acute respiratory syndrome" among hospital workers.
15 March 2003	World Health Organisation (WHO) confirms that Severe Acute Respiratory Syndrome is a worldwide health threat. TV Channels in Beijing are still forbidden to mention the SARS outbreak.
2 April 2003	WHO recommends people should not travel to Hong Kong and Guangdong unless it is really necessary.
5 April 2003	The Chinese Government finally apologises for failing to take action against the SARS virus. "There had not been enough co-operation with the media to control the disease."
26 April 2003	All schools in Beijing closed because of SARS.
28 April 2003	All cinemas, theatres, karaoke bars and internet cafes in Beijing closed because of SARS.

Question 8 (c) (continued)

SOURCE 2

SARS Worldwide – known deaths by July 2003 in selected countries

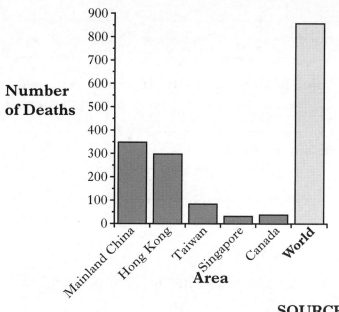

Weekly new SARS cases in China – 2003	
21 April – 28 April	1200
28 April – 5 May	1500
5 May – 12 May	850
12 May – 19 May	400
19 May – 26 May	320
26 May – 2 June	180
2 June – 9 June	40
9 June – 16 June	40
16 June – 23 June	Nil

SOURCE 3

How the Chinese Government and other governments dealt with the SARS outbreak

At the start of April, the World Health Organisation suggested that travellers should avoid Guangdong and Hong Kong and by the end of April they added Beijing to the list. This forced the Chinese Government into action. As a first step, the health minister and the mayor of Beijing were sacked.

As the May Day holiday approached, the Chinese Government organised isolation measures. They ordered anyone who had been in contact with a SARS patient not to leave their own home. Bus and train companies were told to ban any passenger with a cough or a fever. Some hospitals were taken over by the army and shut off from any contact with the outside world. In many areas, free medical treatment was provided to SARS victims. Provinces near seriously affected areas set up roadblocks to stop any infected people getting through.

The World Health Organisation praised Singapore for its speed in reporting SARS cases. To stop anyone with SARS getting into Singapore, technology was used at airports to identify anyone with a high temperature. Early in the outbreak, the Singapore Government gave digital thermometers to school pupils, so they could take their temperature every day and get treatment quickly if necessary. Anyone suspected of having SARS was sent to an isolation hospital. Vietnam was also praised for its open reporting of SARS cases and for its swift action in isolating SARS patients and sealing off affected hospitals.

The Chinese Government was successful in controlling the outbreak of SARS.

A Chinese Communist Party spokesperson

Using Sources 1, 2 and 3, say to what extent the Chinese Communist Party spokesperson is being **selective in the use of facts**.

Your answer must be based entirely on the Sources above and opposite.

(8 marks)

NOW CHECK THAT YOU HAVE ANSWERED ONE QUESTION FROM EACH OF SECTIONS A, B AND C

STUDY THEME 9: ISSUES IN AN EMERGING NATION: SOUTH AFRICA

Question 9

(a) | The South African Government continues to face political opposition.

Describe, **in detail**, the political opposition faced by the South African Government.

(6 marks)

(b) | Crime continues to be a serious problem in South Africa.

Explain, **in detail**, why crime continues to be a major problem in South Africa.

(6 marks)

(c)   Study Sources 1, 2 and 3 below and opposite, then answer the question which follows.

SOURCE 1

Great Strides in Basic Services

South Africa has made great strides in providing basic services such as housing, electricity and water to the people of South Africa, according to a recent report. More than 5 million poor South Africans were provided with housing over a 6 year period with over 1·1 million houses being built. Between 1994 and 2000, 1·5 million new electric connections were installed and an extra 4 million people have access to clean running water.

Critics have pointed out, however, that there remains a backlog of over 7 million people who still need proper shelter. Also black South Africans have less access to piped water than other racial groups. Many people have to use more primitive energy sources for heating and lighting.

Responding to critics, the Minister for Housing said that households in 16 rural development areas will begin receiving 50 kilowatt hours of free electricity. This would give them access to energy for using household goods such as radios, TVs, refrigerators and telephones to which increasing numbers of households have access.

About 23 million people now receive a basic 6 kilolitres of free water per household. In some areas this has not happened especially in rural communities where people do not have access to a water connection. The Government spent Rand 1·1 billion in 2001 to bring water to nearly 1·5 million people.

Question 9 (c) (continued)

SOURCE 2
Main energy sources used for cooking, heating and lighting in South Africa

Cooking   Heating   Lighting

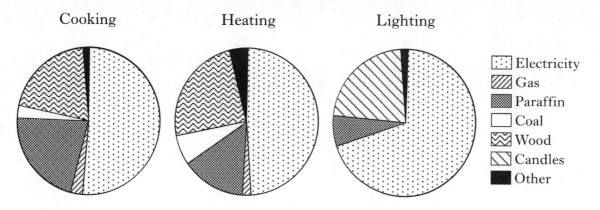

- Electricity
- Gas
- Paraffin
- Coal
- Wood
- Candles
- Other

SOURCE 3
Percentage of households with access to piped water by population group

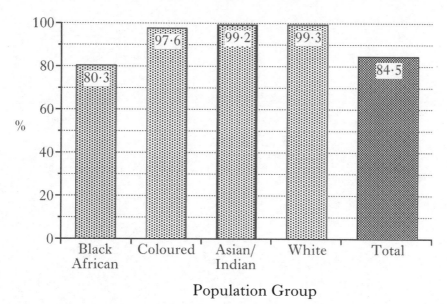

Population Group

The South African Government has been successful in providing basic services to all South African households.

View of Government Official

Using Sources 1, 2 and 3, say to what extent the Government Official is being **selective in the use of facts**.

Your answer must be based entirely on the Sources above and opposite.

(8 marks)

NOW CHECK THAT YOU HAVE ANSWERED ONE QUESTION FROM EACH OF SECTIONS A, B AND C

[END OF QUESTION PAPER]

[BLANK PAGE]

[BLANK PAGE]

X064/201

| NATIONAL QUALIFICATIONS 2006 | MONDAY, 15 MAY 9.00 AM – 11.00 AM | MODERN STUDIES INTERMEDIATE 2 |

This Examination Paper consists of 3 Sections. Within each Section there is a choice of Study Themes. There is one question for each Study Theme.

Section A – Political Issues in the United Kingdom (answer one question)

| Question 1 | Study Theme 1 | Local Government in Scotland | Pages | 3 – 5 |
| Question 2 | Study Theme 2 | Power and Influence in Decision Making | Pages | 7 – 9 |

Section B – Social Issues in the United Kingdom (answer one question)

Question 3	Study Theme 3	Equality in Society: Gender and Race	Pages	11 – 13
Question 4	Study Theme 4	Equality in Society: Health and Wealth	Pages	15 – 17
Question 5	Study Theme 5	Crime and the Law in Society	Pages	19 – 21

Section C – International Issues (answer one question)

Question 6	Study Theme 6	Issues in Europe	Pages	23 – 27
Question 7	Study Theme 7	Issues in an Emerging Nation: Brazil	Pages	28 – 31
Question 8	Study Theme 8	Issues in an Emerging Nation: China	Pages	32 – 35
Question 9	Study Theme 9	Issues in an Emerging Nation: South Africa	Pages	36 – 39

Total Marks – 70

1   Read the questions carefully.

2   You must answer **one** question from **each** of Section A, Section B and Section C.

3   You must answer all parts of the questions you choose.

4   You should spend approximately 40 minutes on each Section.

5   If you cannot do a question or part of a question, move on and try again later.

6   Write your answers in the book provided. Indicate clearly, in the left hand margin, the question and section of question being answered. Do not write in the right hand margin.

SCOTTISH
QUALIFICATIONS
AUTHORITY

[BLANK PAGE]

SECTION A – POLITICAL ISSUES IN THE UNITED KINGDOM

Answer **ONE** question only:

Question 1   Study Theme 1 – Local Government in Scotland on pages 3–5
OR   Question 2   Study Theme 2 – Power and Influence in Decision Making on pages 7–9

STUDY THEME 1: LOCAL GOVERNMENT IN SCOTLAND

Question 1

(*a*)
> Many elderly people need housing specially designed to meet their needs.

Describe, **in detail**, ways in which housing may be specially designed to meet the needs of elderly people.

(6 marks)

(*b*)
> Many people believe that local councillors should be paid for the role they carry out as councillors.

Explain, **in detail**, the reasons why many people believe that local councillors should be paid for the role they carry out as councillors.

(6 marks)

[Turn over

Question 1 (continued)

(c)   Study Sources 1, 2 and 3 below and opposite, then answer the question which follows.

SOURCE 1

MSPs approve new Voting System

A bill has been passed which means the First Past the Post (FPTP) voting system for local elections will be replaced with the proportional Single Transferable Vote (STV) system. The bill passed its final stage in the Scottish Parliament by 96 votes to 18 and the new system will be in place for the next council elections in 2007.

The STV system forms part of the coalition deal struck between Labour and the Liberal Democrats in the Scottish Parliament. The STV system would see the creation of larger wards represented by three or four councillors so voters would have a choice of local councillor to represent them.

Some Labour MSPs said they were opposed to the move, arguing that STV would reduce their party's power and break the link between councillors and the electorate. They have warned that the new system would be confusing for voters. However, the Scottish Executive has promised to help people understand the system through leaflets, education and support and advice at polling stations. It is claimed that there is no need for change; the present system already provides representation for a wide range of parties in local councils.

Supporters of the change to STV say it will lead to more voter interest in council elections resulting in a higher turnout. Voters will have more say over what goes on in their local areas and it will lead to an end of the single party control that exists in many local councils.

SOURCE 2
Political Composition of Selected Local Councils in Scotland
after Election in 2003 using First Past the Post System of Elections

Glasgow City Council	
Party	**Seats**
Labour	71
Liberal Democrats	3
SNP	3
Conservative	1
SSP	1
Labour Control	

Dundee City Council	
Party	**Seats**
Labour	10
Liberal Democrats	2
SNP	11
Conservative	5
Independent	1
No Overall Control; Labour and Liberal Democrat coalition	

Question 1 (c) (continued)

SOURCE 3

Survey of Public Opinion

Question:

Would you like to use the Single Transferable Vote (STV) system of proportional representation for local council elections?

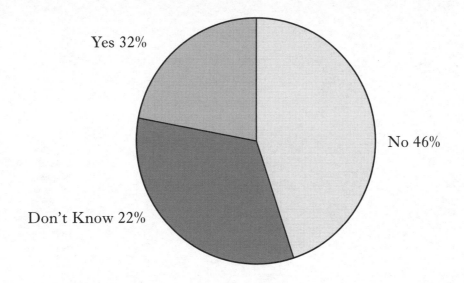

Yes 32%

No 46%

Don't Know 22%

> Introducing the proportional Single Transferable Vote (STV) system for local council elections will improve local government and be popular with voters.

View of Scottish Executive Member

Using Sources 1, 2 and 3, explain why the Scottish Executive Member is being **selective in the use of facts**.

Your answer must be based entirely on the Sources above and opposite.

(8 marks)

NOW GO TO SECTION B ON PAGE 11

[BLANK PAGE]

STUDY THEME 2: POWER AND INFLUENCE IN DECISION MAKING

Question 2

(a) | Pressure groups use a range of methods to try and influence those in power.

Describe, **in detail**, the methods pressure groups use to try and influence those in power.

(6 marks)

(b) | Many people believe that the Scottish Parliament should have more power.

Explain, **in detail**, the reasons why many people believe that the Scottish Parliament should have more power.

(6 marks)

[Turn over

Question 2 (continued)

(c) Study Sources 1, 2 and 3 below and opposite, then answer the question which follows.

SOURCE 1

Representation in the Scottish and UK Parliaments
The Scottish Parliament is elected by a system of proportional representation called the Additional Member System (AMS). The UK Parliament is elected using the First Past the Post (FPTP) system of election.

The Scottish Parliament is elected by a system of proportional representation called the Additional Member System (AMS). The UK Parliament is elected using the First Past the Post (FPTP) system of election.

Under AMS, each voter has two votes and two types of Members of the Scottish Parliament (MSPs) are elected. Each voter has a constituency MSP to represent them and also seven regional MSPs elected from party lists. In the UK Parliament, each constituency has one Member of Parliament (MP) whose role is to represent the whole constituency. Because there is a single MP representing the whole constituency, most voters would know the name of their MP.

Many believe that AMS is more representative because the result of the election is more likely to be a government made up of more than one party. Others believe FPTP is better because a single party government is more likely to be elected and therefore able to put its policies into practice.

In the 2003 election for the Scottish Parliament, 51 female MSPs were elected. This is almost 40% of MSPs; one of the highest figures for female representation in any parliament around the world. In the same election, there were no MSPs elected from ethnic minority communities.

After the election to the House of Commons in 2005, 128 female MPs were elected out of a total of 646, which is 20% of the total. Fifteen ethnic minority MPs were also elected.

SOURCE 2
Political Party Composition of UK and Scottish Parliaments

UK Parliament after 2005 Election		**Scottish Parliament after 2003 Election**	
Party	**MPs**	**Party**	**MSPs**
Labour Party	355	Labour Party	50
Conservative Party	198	Conservative Party	18
Liberal Democrats	62	Liberal Democrats	17
SNP	6	SNP	27
Scottish Socialist Party	0	Scottish Socialist Party	6
Green Party	0	Green Party	7
Other Parties & Independents	25	Other Parties & Independents	4
Total	**646**	**Total**	**129**

- **Labour Government elected**
- **Majority of 64**

- **Labour and Liberal Democrat coalition formed**
- **Majority of 5**

Question 2 (c) (continued)

SOURCE 3

Survey of Public Opinion

Question:

Do you think that the Additional Member System (AMS) is better than First Past the Post (FPTP)?

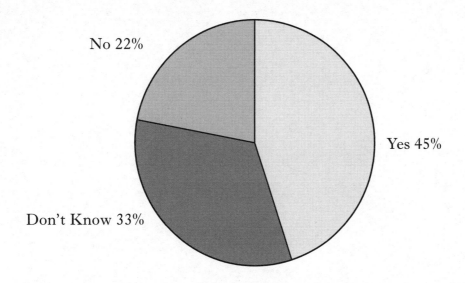

No 22%

Yes 45%

Don't Know 33%

The Additional Member System (AMS), used to elect the Scottish Parliament, is more representative and more popular with voters than the First Past the Post system.

View of Scottish Politician

Using Sources 1, 2 and 3, explain why the Scottish Politician is being **selective in the use of facts**.

Your answer must be based entirely on the Sources above and opposite.

(8 marks)

NOW GO TO SECTION B ON PAGE 11

[BLANK PAGE]

SECTION B – SOCIAL ISSUES IN THE UNITED KINGDOM

Answer **ONE** question only:

       Question 3 Study Theme 3 – Equality in Society: Gender and Race on pages 11–13
OR Question 4 Study Theme 4 – Equality in Society: Health and Wealth on pages 15–17
OR Question 5 Study Theme 5 – Crime and the Law in Society on pages 19–21

STUDY THEME 3: EQUALITY IN SOCIETY: GENDER AND RACE

Question 3

(*a*) | Governments have acted to promote gender and racial equality.

Describe, **in detail**, ways in which governments have acted to promote gender **and/or** racial equality.

(6 marks)

(*b*) | Gender and racial inequalities continue to exist in education in the UK.

Explain, **in detail**, the reasons why gender and racial inequalities continue to exist in education in the UK.

Your answer may refer to gender **or** race **or** both.

(8 marks)

[Turn over

Question 3 (continued)

(c)   Study Sources 1, 2 and 3 below and opposite, then answer the question which follows.

You are an adviser to the Government. You have been asked to recommend whether or not the Equal Pay Act should be strengthened in order to reduce gender inequalities in pay.

Option 1	**Option 2**
Strengthen the Equal Pay Act.	Do not strengthen the Equal Pay Act.

SOURCE 1

Average Weekly Earnings of Full-time Employees by Gender: 1992 to 2002

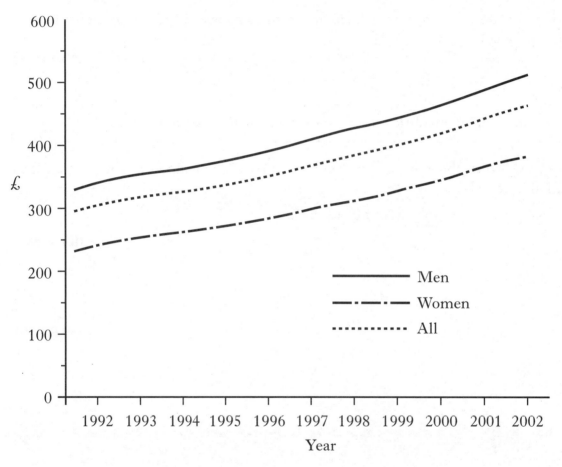

Employees' Average Pay in Great Britain, 2002

	Full-time		Part-time		All Employees	
	Men	**Women**	**Men**	**Women**	**Men**	**Women**
Average yearly earnings	£27 437	£19 811	£9485	£7593	£26 020	£14 619
Increase over year before	4·4%	5·3%	13·9%	9·0%	4·3%	6·0%
Average weekly earnings	£513·80	£383·40	£165·30	£143·80	£484·10	£283·50

Question 3 (c) (continued)

SOURCE 2

Factfile

- Overall, the pay gap between men and women across the UK has increased by 5% over the last 12 months.
- A survey by the GMB union found that, in some regions in Northern Ireland, women's pay was, on average, £38 per week higher than men's. This was due to many men having low paid jobs.
- In Wales, the pay gap has widened, with women earning 23% less than men.
- The Chartered Management Institute's survey of 21 000 managers found, for the first time, that women heading departments earn more than men in the same position. Women average £51 854; men get £1395 less.
- The annual earnings of women working full-time are 72% of men's annual earnings.
- The widest pay difference between men and women was found in the South East of England (30%) and in Scotland (29%).
- The average hourly rate for men went up 2·2% to £12·88, while the rate for women increased by 3·4% to £10·56.

SOURCE 3

Viewpoints

The Equal Pay Act should be strengthened and made more effective. It is disgraceful that the gender pay gap still exists in the 21st century. Employers are not doing enough to bring about equality. Employers should be forced by law to carry out pay reviews. More research into why women are stuck in low paid, part-time jobs, would highlight issues such as the lack of childcare facilities. It may also show that women are still expected to be the main carers of children.

Rachel Townsend, spokesperson for equal pay group

Changing the Equal Pay Act would damage British industry and raise the unemployment rate. British industry needs to compete in an international economy and offer quality products at competitive prices. It would be unable to do this if more laws were introduced to increase wages. British businesses cannot be held responsible for gender divisions in society. The education system is what needs to be changed so that women are more able to enter the job market for higher paid jobs such as engineering and computing.

Jack Digby, spokesperson for British businesses

You must recommend whether to strengthen the Equal Pay Act (Option 1), **or** not to strengthen the Equal Pay Act (Option 2), in order to reduce gender inequalities in pay.

Using Sources 1, 2 and 3 above and opposite, **which option would you recommend**?

Give reasons to **support** your choice.

In your answer you must say why you **did not recommend the other option.**

Your answer must be based on all the Sources.   **(10 marks)**

NOW GO TO SECTION C ON PAGE 23

[BLANK PAGE]

STUDY THEME 4: EQUALITY IN SOCIETY: HEALTH AND WEALTH

Question 4

(*a*) | Government policies have helped to promote health and reduce poverty in Scotland. |

Describe, **in detail**, ways in which government policies have helped to promote health **and/or** reduce poverty in Scotland.

(6 marks)

(*b*) | Inequalities continue to exist in health and wealth in the UK. |

Explain, **in detail**, the reasons why inequalities continue to exist in health and wealth in the UK.

Your answer may refer to health **or** wealth **or** both.

(8 marks)

[Turn over

Question 4 (continued)

(c)   Study Sources 1, 2 and 3 below and opposite, then answer the question which follows.

You are an adviser to the Scottish Executive. You have been asked to recommend whether or not to continue the ban on smoking in enclosed public places in order to improve health.

Option 1	**Option 2**
Continue the ban on smoking in enclosed public places.	Do not continue the ban on smoking in enclosed public places.

SOURCE 1
Percentage (%) of Adult Population that Smokes

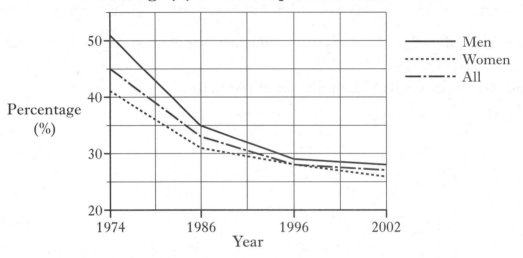

Results of a Health Survey of Parents with Children under 10 Years of Age

Does passive smoking result in the following health problems in children?	Percentage (%) saying "Yes"
Asthma	26%
Lung infections	22%
Cancer	11%
Coughs/sore throat	5%
Bronchitis	5%

Number of Deaths from Selected Causes Linked to Smoking and Passive Smoking in Scotland per Year

Cause of Death	Total Deaths	Deaths linked to smoking	Deaths linked to passive smoking
Lung cancer	4000	3123	44
Heart disease	11 700	3767	395
Stroke	6750	1540	335
Respiratory	6500	2700	91
Total	**28 950**	**11 130**	**865**

Question 4 (c) (continued)

SOURCE 2

Selected Facts and Viewpoints

- 17 000 children under the age of five are admitted to hospital every year with illnesses resulting from passive smoking.
- The UK Government earned around £9616 million in revenue from tobacco taxes and VAT in 2003.
- Smoking kills 114 000 people every year in the UK.
- 25% of smokers said they would avoid places where the ban was in force.
- A six-month ban on smoking in public places in an American town reduced the number of heart attacks by almost 50%.
- In a survey, seven out of ten people did not support a ban on smoking in pubs, restaurants and clubs.
- It has been found that a smoke-free environment encourages smokers to reduce the number of cigarettes smoked or to quit altogether.
- In a survey, 66% agreed that the decision to allow or not to allow smoking in enclosed public places should be left up to the business owners.
- Passive smoking is thought to cause hundreds of deaths every year in the UK.

SOURCE 3

Viewpoints

The ban on smoking in enclosed public places is not only a restriction of human rights it is also having a damaging effect on the profits of pubs and restaurants and causing job losses. Pub and restaurant owners should decide for themselves if they want to impose a ban. However, it has been found that banning smoking rarely makes financial sense. People are sick of being "nannied" by the state with more and more laws being introduced preventing them from making choices about how they want to live their lives.

Richard Wright, restaurant owner

As a bar worker, I used to be exposed to other people's smoke throughout my working day. My clothes smelled and I suffered many colds and sore throats. Bar work provides a valuable source of income for thousands of young people trying to help pay for their studies. It is unjust and a restriction of our human rights to risk suffering lung disease in later life. Governments have a duty to pass laws to protect workers and the public.

Reo Lazos, bar worker

You must recommend whether to continue the ban on smoking in enclosed public places (Option 1), **or** not to continue the ban on smoking in enclosed public places (Option 2), in order to improve health.

Using Sources 1, 2 and 3 above and opposite, **which option would you recommend**?

Give reasons to **support** your choice.

In your answer you must say why you **did not recommend the other option**.

Your answer must be based on all the Sources.

(10 marks)

NOW GO TO SECTION C ON PAGE 23

[BLANK PAGE]

STUDY THEME 5: CRIME AND THE LAW IN SOCIETY

Question 5

(*a*) | The Children's Panel deals with some of the problems faced by young people.

Describe, **in detail**, ways in which the Children's Panel deals with some of the problems faced by young people.

(6 marks)

(*b*) | Some parts of Scotland have higher crime rates than others.

Explain, **in detail**, the reasons why some parts of Scotland have higher crime rates than others.

(8 marks)

[Turn over

Question 5 (continued)

(c)   Study Sources 1, 2 and 3 below and opposite, then answer the question which follows.

You are an adviser to the Scottish Executive. You have been asked to recommend whether or not to allow the electronic tagging of young people under 16 years of age in order to reduce the number of crimes committed by young people.

Option 1	**Option 2**
Allow electronic tagging of young people under 16 years of age.	Do not allow electronic tagging of young people under 16 years of age.

SOURCE 1

Statistics on Crime

Individuals per 10 000 of the population with one or more convictions for a crime by gender and age in Scotland

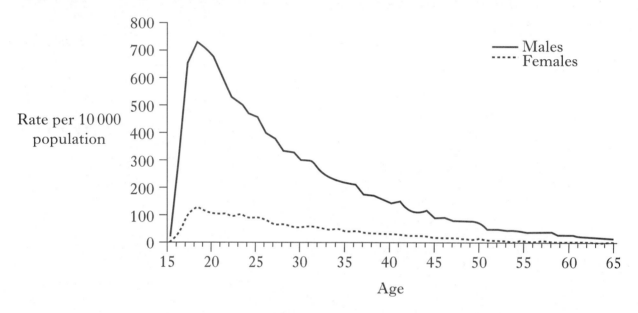

Result of opinion poll

Should non-violent offenders, under 16, be electronically tagged or kept in secure accommodation?

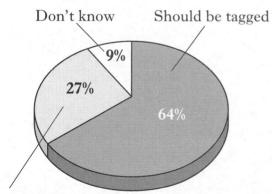

Results of a survey carried out in a housing estate affected by the anti-social behaviour of young people.	Yes
Have you been verbally abused?	49%
Have you suffered vandalism to property?	45%
Have you been intimidated by local youths?	38%
Have you been the victim of theft?	31%

Question 5 (*c*) (continued)

SOURCE 2

Selected Facts and Viewpoints

- There are around one million young people under 16 in Scotland and only 1·4% are referred to the Children's Panel for offending.
- Since 1991, assaults have risen by 33% from 41 022 to 54 726.
- The percentage of young offenders has decreased by 19% over the last three years.
- Over the past 10 years, the number of breaches of the peace has risen by 34%.
- An estimated 50% of young people aged 12–15 were the victims of at least one crime in the last year.
- Most children who do offend grow out of it.
- An MSP says that three-quarters of the issues raised by constituents are about anti-social behaviour.
- The electronic tag may quickly become a status symbol or badge of honour without tackling the problems for which it was provided in the first place.

SOURCE 3

Viewpoints

The electronic tagging of people, especially those under 16, is a breach of human rights and has no place in a modern society. Community-based programmes aimed at tackling the causes of youth crime have been successful. Many more of these programmes need to be introduced, especially in areas of high unemployment and poverty. Most of the young people who display anti-social behaviour are very vulnerable and would be further damaged psychologically by such harsh methods of punishment.

George Dickson, community youth worker

Electronic tagging will shift the responsibility for the behaviour of children back onto their parents and help to rid our communities of rising anti-social behaviour. Criminal behaviour in the under-16 age group is a serious issue. The Scottish Executive must put in place punishments that are an effective alternative to residential care. It costs taxpayers less and allows young people to stay at home. Electronic tagging is better than placing youngsters in secure accommodation and could be in the best interests of the offender.

Judith Forsythe, police spokesperson

You must recommend whether to allow electronic tagging of young people under 16 years of age (Option 1), **or** not to allow electronic tagging of young people under 16 years of age (Option 2), in order to reduce the number of crimes committed by young people.

Using Sources 1, 2 and 3 above and opposite, **which option would you recommend**?

Give reasons to **support** your choice.

In your answer you must say why you **did not recommend the other option**.

Your answer must be based on all the Sources.

(10 marks)

NOW GO TO SECTION C ON PAGE 23

[BLANK PAGE]

SECTION C – INTERNATIONAL ISSUES

Answer **ONE** question only:

Question 6 Study Theme 6 – Issues in Europe on pages 23–27
OR Question 7 Study Theme 7 – Issues in an Emerging Nation: Brazil on pages 28–31
OR Question 8 Study Theme 8 – Issues in an Emerging Nation: China on pages 32–35
OR Question 9 Study Theme 9 – Issues in an Emerging Nation: South Africa
on pages 36–39

STUDY THEME 6: ISSUES IN EUROPE

Question 6

(*a*)

> NATO has helped keep the peace in Europe in recent years.

Describe, **in detail**, **two** ways in which NATO has helped keep the peace in Europe in recent years.

(4 marks)

(*b*)

> Many members of the European Union (EU) have joined the Single European Currency (Euro).

Explain, **in detail**, the reasons why many members of the European Union (EU) have joined the Single European Currency (Euro).

(6 marks)

[Turn over

Question 6 (continued)

(c)   Study Sources 1, 2 and 3 below and opposite, then answer the question which follows.

SOURCE 1

Percentage (%) change in serious crimes recorded by the police in selected countries in western Europe, 1996–2000

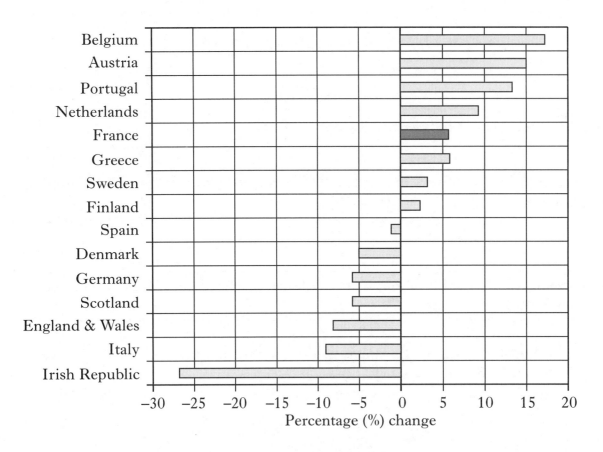

SOURCE 2

Numbers of crimes recorded by the police in selected countries in western Europe, 2001

Crime	United Kingdom	Germany	Italy	France
Murder	1050	868	785	1047
Violent crime	870 633	188 413	719 119	279 324
Motor vehicle theft	362 990	121 533	202 428	414 983
Domestic burglary	469 617	133 722	184 512	210 850
Drug trafficking	30 148	79 787	26 796	4047

Question 6 (*c*) (continued)

SOURCE 3

Concerns about Violent Crime and Drugs, 2003

The United Kingdom has the worst record in western Europe for murder, violence and burglary. People in the UK are more likely to be the victims of violent crime than people in any other country in the industrialised world. Violent crime in the UK is three times the level of the next highest country in western Europe.

The total number of crimes recorded in Germany was over 6 million, the highest in Europe. Half of all crimes in Germany are drug-related.

In Italy, a lot of crimes are also drug-related. There is concern that drug gangs are becoming more powerful. This makes it more difficult to maintain law and order.

Total crimes in France reached over 4 million for the first time in 2003, an increase of nearly 8% from the previous year. The largest increase was in violent crime, up by nearly 10%. Experts say that the increase in crime in France is due to young people who have dropped out of the education system and are unemployed. They express their anger by burning cars in the city centres.

> France has very serious problems of crime compared with other countries in western Europe.

View of European crime reporter

Using Sources 1, 2 and 3 above and opposite, give **two** reasons to **support** and **two** reasons to **oppose** the view of the European crime reporter.

Your answer must be based entirely on the Sources above and opposite.

(8 marks)

[Turn over

Question 6 (continued)

(*d*)   Study Sources 1, 2 and 3 below and opposite, then answer the question which follows.

SOURCE 1

Selected Statistics for the United Kingdom and Romania

	United Kingdom	**Romania**
Population	59 068 000	22 387 000
Life expectancy	78 years	71 years
Child mortality*—male	7 per 1000	22 per 1000
Child mortality*—female	6 per 1000	19 per 1000
Government spending on health	$1 508 per person	$93 per person
Public spending on education	4·4% of GDP**	3·5% of GDP**
Spending on research	1·9% of GDP**	0·4% of GDP**
Unemployment rate	3·4%	7·3%

*   **Child mortality**—probability of dying under 5 years of age
****GDP**—measure of wealth produced by a country in a year

SOURCE 2

Opportunities in the United Kingdom—Case Study: Coventry

A new youth centre has been opened in the Foleshill area of Coventry by Advantage West Midlands, the government regional development agency and Youth First, a local voluntary organisation. It has a recording studio and editing suite. The aim is to boost the confidence of young people to help them get a career in the media. Coventry City Council is responsible for the day-to-day running of the centre.

Youth Training and the New Deal for Young People are government schemes available for school leavers. Many students in Coventry go on to college or university. Government grants are available for students from poorer families to make sure they are able to continue with their studies.

Many people in Coventry earn well above the UK average monthly wage of £1524. There are a range of jobs in Coventry. Traditionally, Coventry has been the home of the car industry. There are also job opportunities in electronics and aerospace. More recently, call centres have been attracted to the city. Jobs in this sector are threatened, however, as many call centre companies are considering relocation to India where pay rates are much lower. The higher than average level of unemployment in Coventry has led to an increase in stress related illnesses.

Question 6 (*d*) (continued)

SOURCE 3

Opportunities in Romania—Case Study: Timisoara

The Rudolph Walter Centre in the city of Timisoara is home and school to 250 orphans, street children and young people with disabilities. The Romanian Government cannot afford to run orphanages so the Centre gets food, medical supplies and books from charities and church groups in other European countries and the USA.

Young people can only stay in the Centre till they are 18. Most leave with no home and no job. Many then live on the streets and turn to crime and prostitution. They face serious mental health problems. The UN World Bank gives money to help improve the lives of Timisoara's street children. There are no government training schemes. A few foreign charities provide education and training for work.

The unemployment rate in Timisoara is only 3%. Employment prospects are good for young people with qualifications but only the most advantaged young people can go to university. European and American firms have been attracted to Timisoara because wage costs are low. The average wage in Romania is only £50 per month. There are a variety of jobs in firms involved in engineering, telecommunications and information technology. Some of the most highly qualified young people leave Romania for jobs in electronic firms in the USA, where they will earn high wages and have a good standard of living.

Using Sources 1, 2 and 3, what **conclusions** can be reached about life in the UK compared with life in Romania?

You should reach conclusions about at least **three** of the following:

- health
- employment and unemployment
- help provided for young people
- education and training.

You must use information from all of the Sources above and opposite. You should compare information within and between the Sources.

(8 marks)

NOW CHECK THAT YOU HAVE ANSWERED ONE QUESTION FROM EACH OF SECTIONS A, B AND C.

STUDY THEME 7: ISSUES IN AN EMERGING NATION: BRAZIL

Question 7

(*a*) | Native Indians and street children have made progress in Brazil in recent years. |

Describe, **in detail**, **two** ways Native Indians **and/or** street children have made progress in Brazil in recent years.

(4 marks)

(*b*) | The Brazilian Government has had to deal with a number of economic problems in recent years. |

Explain, **in detail**, the reasons why the Brazilian Government has had to deal with economic problems in recent years.

(6 marks)

(*c*) Study Sources 1, 2 and 3 below and opposite, then answer the question which follows.

SOURCE 1

Number of Crimes Reported to the Police in Brazil

	2001	2002
Murder	39 618	39 805
Rape	14 653	14 534
Serious assault	1043	1641
Theft	534 234	536 642
Car theft	152 572	153 890
Fraud	119 661	117 594
Drug offences	79 803	78 985
Total	941 584	943 091

Question 7 (c) (continued)

SOURCE 2

Murders by Location in São Paulo City, 1998–2000

Location of murder	Average number of victims per month		
	1998	**1999**	**2000**
Bar or cafeteria	116	130	124
Gas station	13	9	7
Bus stop or terminal	8	6	10
Terrace house	153	128	140
Apartment or office building	7	7	4
Favela	77	71	77
Street	560	678	730

SOURCE 3

Violent Crime in Brazil's Cities

A recent study of crime in Brazil concludes that large numbers of young people under the age of 18 are killed by guns each year in Rio de Janeiro. Many slums in Rio de Janeiro are run by drug lords who employ teenagers to protect their areas. In the last 14 years, firearms in Rio alone killed almost 4000 young people. Most of the killings are about disputes over territory between drug gangs. There are similar levels of violence in other Brazilian cities, such as São Paulo. Brazilian cities have some of the highest murder rates in the world. In rural areas of Brazil, however, levels of crime are not a major problem. Critics argue that the Government is not doing enough to tackle the violence in the cities.

The Brazilian Justice Minister recently announced an agreement to give almost $15 million in aid to Rio de Janeiro. The money would be used to create a new elite police unit as well as to strengthen existing police forces. This may go some way to reduce violent crime. In the favelas, tens of thousands of people are shot dead each year. The Brazilian Senate has passed a bill to outlaw the carrying of guns in public and control illegal gun ownership. The legal age for owning a gun is being raised from 21 to 25 years.

The Government has been successful in dealing with crime in Brazil.

View of a Government spokesperson

Using Sources 1, 2 and 3 above and opposite, give **two** reasons to **support** and **two** reasons to **oppose** the view of the Government spokesperson.

Your answer must be based entirely on the Sources above and opposite.

(8 marks)

[Turn over

Question 7 (continued)

(*d*)   Study Sources 1, 2 and 3 below and opposite, then answer the question which follows.

SOURCE 1

> ### Health in Brazil
>
> Some regions of Brazil have poorer health rates compared to others. The North East, for example, has sickness patterns which are similar to those of the most deprived countries in Africa and Asia, whereas the South, South East and the Federal District have similar health conditions to those of many developed countries. Malaria is still a problem in the Amazon region. Infant mortality rates also vary across the regions. In the North, it is 64 deaths per 1000 compared to 23 per 1000 in the South East. The infant mortality rate, although still very high, is much lower than it was in the 1940s.
>
> In many regions, women's health is a problem. The mortality rate for mothers is 150 deaths for every 100 000 births. Around 5000 women die every year due to pregnancy or childbirth complications resulting in between 9000 and 15 000 children becoming orphans. High blood pressure is the main cause of death, followed by haemorrhages, infections and abortions. Every 24 minutes, there is a new case of breast cancer. There is very little preventive medicine and 60% of the women discover the disease when it is already advanced.
>
> There are also differences in health between rich and poor. The poor die on average 10 years younger than the rich. This is linked to bad living conditions. Many live in favelas where there are few public services and little access to good health care.

SOURCE 2

Percentage (%) of Children under 2 years immunised against selected Diseases

Year	TB	Diphtheria	Polio	Measles	Hepatitis
2000	89%	88%	93%	91%	85%
2001	92%	90%	95%	96%	92%
2002	96%	95%	97%	98%	92%
2003	99%	96%	99%	99%	91%

Question 7 (*d*) (continued)

SOURCE 3

Health Care Inequalities in Brazil

Research has shown that the number of deaths related to pregnancy, childbirth, and postnatal* complications among women is three times greater in areas which lack prenatal** care. In the North East, a higher percentage of expectant mothers failed to receive prenatal care compared with the Northern Region.

Access to health care also results in differences in infant and child mortality rates. The poorest sections of the Brazilian population, living in areas which lack access to health care, have poorer housing, lack basic sanitation and have higher child mortality levels.

There are also differences in the provision of health services between rich and poor people in Brazil. Most people in Brazil cannot afford private health care. Only 26% of the population of Brazil is covered by private health care insurance.

In Rio, for example, the contrast is evident when comparing the life of two families. Andre Coneicao is 29 years old and makes $200 a month as a night guard. He lives at the Rocinha favela in a four-room shack with 22 relatives, including his mother, children and nephews. The family cannot afford private health care and have to rely on public health clinics that lack staff and medical equipment. Many people wait long hours for treatment. The clinics are unable to deal with many illnesses due to lack of resources. Carlos Penna, aged 51 years, earns $2000 a month. He lives in an affluent area in a four-bedroom house with a swimming pool. He and his wife have private health insurance and go to a private clinic to have regular health checks. If they become ill, they do not have to wait for treatment and have access to medicines, modern equipment and well-trained staff.

* postnatal–after the birth
** prenatal–before the birth

Using Sources 1, 2 and 3, what **conclusions** can be reached about health in Brazil?

You should reach conclusions about at least **three** of the following:

- health of children
- health of women
- health of rich and poor
- regional health comparisons.

You must use information from all of the Sources above and opposite. You should compare information within and between the Sources.

(8 marks)

NOW CHECK THAT YOU HAVE ANSWERED ONE QUESTION FROM EACH OF SECTIONS A, B AND C.

STUDY THEME 8: ISSUES IN AN EMERGING NATION: CHINA

Question 8

(*a*)

> Freedom of expression is limited in China.

Describe, **in detail**, **two** ways in which freedom of expression is limited in China.

(4 marks)

(*b*)

> Many foreign businesses have been attracted to China in recent years.

Explain, **in detail**, the reasons why many foreign businesses have been attracted to China in recent years.

(6 marks)

(*c*) Study Sources 1, 2 and 3 below and opposite, then answer the question which follows.

SOURCE 1

Factfile – Crime in China

- In China, many crimes are punished by death including bribery, drug dealing, stealing petrol and violent crime.

- China is only fourteenth in the world for the number of executions per million people.

- In the first three months of 2004 there were 923 000 criminal cases reported in China, a 14·2% increase over the same period in 2003.

- Police were successful in clearing up 285 000 cases in the first three months of 2004. This was 1·6% higher than at the start of 2003.

- There were 639 theft cases in the first three months of 2004. An increase of 17·1% over the same time in 2003.

- Following the murder of four students in Guangxi province, police tracked down the criminal and arrested him within 3 weeks.

- One man was accused of 65 cases of murder in 2003. Police were criticised for keeping the case secret instead of asking the public for help.

Question 8 (*c*) (continued)

SOURCE 2

Number of Executions in Selected Countries, 2002

Country	Number of executions	Number of executions per million people
China	1067	0·82 per million
Democratic Republic of Congo	100	1·76 per million
United States	68	0·23 per million
Iran	66	0·96 per million
Egypt	48	0·64 per million
Belarus	33	3·19 per million
Taiwan	32	1·41 per million

SOURCE 3

Dealing with Drug Addiction in Yunnan Province

South-West China's Yunnan province has China's biggest drug problem. The authorities argue that the province's 41 million people are innocent victims of the international trade in heroin. Four-fifths of China's opium seizures are in Yunnan province. Along the drug supply routes, cases of drug addiction and HIV/AIDS have increased.

In Yunnan, a mixture of tactics is used to fight the drug problem. Tough tactics are used against drug dealers. About 400 drug dealers are executed each year in the province. Also in Yunnan, an unusual experiment has taken place. Rehabilitation centres have been set up with the emphasis on prevention and cure. In contrast, police in the rest of China treat addicts as criminals. Addicts picked up for the first time in Yunnan are sent for 3 months' detoxification in special centres. This involves using herbal pills, counselling and the discipline of an army camp. The police in Yunnan say that there is a need for community care and counselling when addicts return home. They also call for education programmes at school. Centres in Yunnan have a caring approach which has had considerable success in keeping people off drugs.

China is harsh and effective in its treatment of criminals.

View of a Chinese crime researcher

Using Sources 1, 2 and 3 above and opposite, give **two** reasons to **support** and **two** reasons to **oppose** the view of the Chinese crime researcher.

Your answer must be based entirely on the Sources above and opposite.

(8 marks)

[Turn over

Question 8 (continued)

(*d*)   Study Sources 1, 2 and 3 below and opposite, then answer the question which follows.

SOURCE 1

Selected Health Statistics in China and the World

		China	World Average
Percentage (%) of population using treated drinking water	Urban	94%	95%
	Rural	66%	71%
Percentage (%) of population using adequate sanitation facilities	Urban	69%	85%
	Rural	27%	40%
Births attended by trained medical staff		70%	57%

	Year	China	World Average
Child (under 5) mortality rate per 10 000	1960	225	NA
	1990	49	NA
	2002	39	83

NA—figures not available

Life expectancy in China	
1970	61 years
2002	71 years

Percentage (%) of births in hospital in China 2002	
Urban	91%
Rural	32%

Percentage (%) of Chinese population living in urban and rural areas

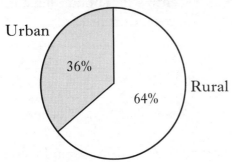

Urban 36%
Rural 64%

Percentage (%) of Chinese health spending in urban and rural areas

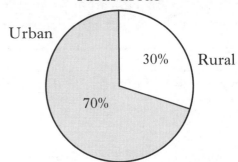

Urban 70%
Rural 30%

Question 8 (d) (continued)

SOURCE 2

Health Care in China

Many young children have died from malnutrition in China. The cause was a cheap brand of fake baby milk powder. Many parents had not realised that their children were so ill and put off taking them to hospital because treatment is so expensive.

Rongrong was only a few weeks old when her parents noticed she was unwell. They took her to a village clinic then to a rural hospital. Both failed to see that she was severely malnourished. It cost her father the equivalent of two and a half month's salary. When her parents eventually took her to a city hospital, they found out what was wrong. After seven days and hospital bills costing another three months' salary, Rongrong died.

There are huge differences in the health of people in different regions. In rural areas like the province of Anhui where Rongrong was born, millions of people have died because they cannot afford health care. A government survey found that 60% of rural residents avoid hospital altogether because of the cost. In rich areas, for example around Shanghai, there are good health facilities. Many people are well paid and can afford to pay for treatment. The health of people in the coastal provinces is as good as in many western countries.

SOURCE 3

Health Care in Beijing

Poor migrant workers in Beijing welcome the chance to buy stale rice at half the price of normal rice. It is mouldy and tastes bad but a portion can be bought for 5 Yuan. Eating stale rice may result in sickness. In the long term, workers who eat mouldy rice may develop cancer of the lungs or kidneys. Buying stale rice and selling it is against the law.

Private firms can now set up private hospitals. People in Beijing who can afford treatment can get it at the Homecare Women and Children's Hospital, a Chinese-American joint venture. Standards of care are as high as in many hospitals in Europe or the USA. People have to pay for treatment in these hospitals just as they do in public hospitals. The difference is that they will not be covered by the public health insurance scheme. So they will not be able to claim back the cost of treatment. Only families with a high income can afford to use these private hospitals.

Using Sources 1, 2 and 3, what **conclusions** can be reached about health in China?

You should reach conclusions about at least **three** of the following:

- health of babies and young children
- health in urban and rural areas
- health of rich and poor
- international health comparisons.

You must use information from all of the Sources above and opposite. You should compare information within and between the Sources.

(8 marks)

NOW CHECK THAT YOU HAVE ANSWERED ONE QUESTION FROM EACH OF SECTIONS A, B AND C.

STUDY THEME 9: ISSUES IN AN EMERGING NATION: SOUTH AFRICA

Question 9

(*a*)

> The South African Government is dealing with health problems in South Africa.

Describe, **in detail**, **two** ways the South African Government is dealing with health problems in South Africa.

(4 marks)

(*b*)

> Economic inequalities continue to exist in South Africa.

Explain, **in detail**, the reasons why economic inequalities continue to exist in South Africa.

(6 marks)

(*c*) Study Sources 1, 2 and 3 below and opposite, then answer the question which follows.

SOURCE 1

**Changes in recorded Murder Rate 1994–2003
by Province (per 100 000)**

Murders per 100 000 (y-axis)

Provinces (x-axis: Limpopo, North West, Mpumalanga, Free State, Eastern Cape, Northern Cape, KwaZulu Natal, Gauteng, Western Cape)

Legend: 1994, 2003

Question 9 (c) (continued)

SOURCE 2

Changes in the Amount of Selected Crimes in South Africa 2002–2003

Crime	2002	2003
Murder	21 405	21 553
Attempted murder	31 293	35 861
Robbery	116 736	126 905
Rape	54 293	52 425
Common assault	261 886	282 526
Drug related crime	52 900	53 810
Carjacking	15 846	14 691

SOURCE 3

Crime in South Africa

Crime is still a major problem in South Africa according to a recent crime report. In Gauteng Province alone, 5000 murders and 10 000 rapes are committed each year. The vast majority of these crimes are not committed in the prosperous suburbs but in the poor black townships. In the wealthy, mostly white, suburbs, you will see high walls and electric fences surrounding houses – most have alarm systems, metal grilles and infra-red sensors. Some black commentators complain that violent crime has not significantly worsened in recent years. It is just getting more publicity and white people are much more aware of it for the first time.

The Government has hit back at reports that violent crime is still a major problem. A report published by the Department of Health stated that Gauteng has experienced a decrease of 21·8% in violent deaths between 1996 and 2003, including a decrease in firearm related deaths. Violence related injuries were also on the decrease. A Johannesburg doctor said, "We are winning in our efforts to make Gauteng a better place to live." However, a journalist has claimed that the recent crime figures are not accurate and have been altered to make the Government's record on crime look better.

There has been little improvement in levels of crime across South Africa.

View of opposition party spokesperson

Using Sources 1, 2 and 3 above and opposite, give **two** reasons to **support** and **two** reasons to **oppose** the view of the opposition party spokesperson.

Your answer must be based entirely on the Sources above and opposite.

(8 marks)

[Turn over

Question 9 (continued)

(*d*)   Study Sources 1, 2 and 3 below and opposite, then answer the question which follows.

SOURCE 1

National Assembly Election Results, 1999 and 2004

Party	1999 Votes (%)	1999 Seats	2004 Votes (%)	2004 Seats
African National Congress (ANC)	66·3%	266	69·6%	279
Democratic Alliance (DA)	9·5%	38	12·3%	50
New National Party (NNP)	6·9%	28	1·7%	7
Inkatha Freedom Party (IFP)	6·6%	34	6·9%	28
United Democratic Movement (UDM)	3·4%	14	2·3%	9
African Christian Democratic Party (ACDP)	1·4%	6	1·6%	6
Freedom Front (FF)	0·8%	3	0·9%	4
Pan Africanist Congress (PAC)	0·7%	3	0·7%	3
Others	4·4%	8	4·0%	14
Total	**100%**	**400**	**100%**	**400**
Number of registered voters	18 172 751		20 674 926	
Voter turnout	89·3%		76·7%	

SOURCE 2

Provincial Seats Won, 2004

Region \ Party	ANC	DA	NNP	IFP	UDM	ACDP	FF	PAC	Others
Eastern Cape	51	5	0	0	6	0	0	1	0
Free State	25	3	0	0	0	1	1	0	0
Gauteng	51	15	0	2	1	1	1	1	1
KwaZulu Natal	38	7	0	30	1	2	0	0	2
Mpumalanga	27	2	0	0	0	0	1	0	0
Northern Cape	21	3	2	0	0	1	1	0	2
Limpopo	45	2	0	0	1	1	0	0	0
North West	27	2	0	0	0	0	1	0	3
Western Cape	19	12	5	0	1	2	0	0	3
A report compiled by the Election Observer Mission (EOM) said that the elections were, on the whole, conducted in a peaceful, orderly and open manner.									

Question 9 (d) (continued)

SOURCE 3

South Africa Elections

In South Africa, the ANC celebrated another victory in the 2004 general election which was declared free and fair. The ANC won the majority of seats in the National Assembly, obtaining its first ever two-thirds majority. It also did very well in the provincial elections winning KwaZulu Natal and Western Cape for the first time. The ANC's majority has also increased at national level. The Election Observer Mission (EOM) concluded that the elections were a true reflection of the will of the people of South Africa. President Thabo Mbeki also congratulated all political parties who contested the election and thanked them for readily accepting the final results "even in those instances in which the outcome was not as favourable as they might have expected." The President expressed relief at the fact that political tensions in KwaZulu Natal did not spoil the election. The EOM did note that the conduct of the elections in a few areas had some problems, mostly involving inconsistent voting and counting procedures. For example, some voting stations used one ballot box for both national and provincial ballot papers whilst others used a ballot box each for the two different papers.

A high voter turnout contradicted the predictions of voter apathy. People queued in their millions to vote in the country's third general election since the fall of apartheid. The electoral commission reported a strong turnout at most of the country's 17 000 polling stations. In some areas, people had queued from 3 am. The Western Cape and KwaZulu Natal recorded the two lowest provincial turnouts where it had been expected to be higher due to the contest between the ANC and the opposition parties.

Using Sources 1, 2 and 3, what **conclusions** can be reached about the elections in South Africa?

You should reach conclusions about at least **three** of the following:

- support for political parties at national level
- support for political parties at provincial level
- voter turnout and registration
- the conduct of the elections.

You must use information from all of the Sources above and opposite. You should compare information within and between the Sources.

(8 marks)

NOW CHECK THAT YOU HAVE ANSWERED ONE QUESTION FROM EACH OF SECTIONS A, B AND C.

[END OF QUESTION PAPER]

[BLANK PAGE]

[BLANK PAGE]

X236/201

NATIONAL
QUALIFICATIONS
2007

TUESDAY, 22 MAY
9.00 AM – 11.00 AM

MODERN STUDIES
INTERMEDIATE 2

This Examination Paper consists of 3 Sections. Within each Section there is a choice of Study Themes. There is one question for each Study Theme.

Section A – Political Issues in the United Kingdom (answer one question)

Section B – Social Issues in the United Kingdom (answer one question)

Section C – International Issues (answer one question)

Total Marks – 70

1 Read the questions carefully.

2 You must answer **one** question from **each** of Section A, Section B and Section C.

3 You must answer **all** parts of the questions you choose. Questions in Section A each have four parts; questions in Sections B and C each have three parts.

4 You should spend approximately 40 minutes on each Section.

5 If you cannot do a question or part of a question, move on and try again later.

6 Write your answers in the book provided. Indicate clearly, in the left hand margin, the question and section of question being answered. Do not write in the right hand margin.

SCOTTISH
QUALIFICATIONS
AUTHORITY

©

[BLANK PAGE]

SECTION A – POLITICAL ISSUES IN THE UNITED KINGDOM

Answer **ONE** question only:

      Question 1 Study Theme 1A – Government and Decision Making in Scotland

                                                            on pages 3–7

OR   Question 2 Study Theme 1B – Government and Decision Making in Central Government

                                                            on pages 9–13

STUDY THEME 1A: GOVERNMENT AND DECISION MAKING IN SCOTLAND

Question 1

(*a*) | MSPs can represent their constituents in the Scottish Parliament in a number of ways. |

Describe, **in detail**, **two** ways MSPs can represent their constituents in the Scottish Parliament.

                                                                    (4 marks)

(*b*) | The Scottish Executive has been made up of a coalition of two parties since 1999. |

Explain, **in detail**, why some people believe a coalition is a good way of governing Scotland.

                                                                     (6 marks)

[Turn over

Question 1 (continued)

(c)   Study Sources 1, 2 and 3 below and opposite, then answer the question which follows.

SOURCE 1

Make Poverty History Campaign

The Make Poverty History Campaign organised a demonstration to put pressure on the leaders of the eight richest countries in the world, known as G8. The demonstration, which took place in July 2005 in Edinburgh, was one of the largest ever in Scotland. It aimed to influence the G8 leaders meeting in nearby Gleneagles.

The leaders would be meeting to consider aid, trade and debt relief for the poorest nations in the world. Almost a quarter of a million people from all walks of life and from all over the UK came to Edinburgh to tell the G8 leaders that real action must be taken to reduce poverty around the world. First Minister, Jack McConnell and Chancellor of the Exchequer, Gordon Brown, both attended the demonstration and expressed their support for the campaign.

The demonstration was made up of young, middle-aged and older people, members of trade unions, church groups and anti-poverty organisations. On a sunny day, the thousands attending listened to speeches and music and marched around Edinburgh getting their message across to the newspapers and television broadcasters who covered the event.

It was a pity that many of the reports the next day focussed upon the small group of radical protesters who threatened to break away from the official demonstration and cause violence and damage.

SOURCE 2

Direct Action at G8 Summit

As the leaders of the G8 countries met behind a ring of steel at Gleneagles Hotel, violence erupted outside. Dozens of protesters disrupted traffic across Scotland by sitting down in the middle of motorways and blocking railway lines. A few attacked buildings and cars in nearby Stirling, leading to violent confrontations with the police.

Later that day, as the protest march at Gleneagles came to an end, a few hundred protesters tried to break down the steel fence surrounding the hotel. Hundreds of police were moved into the area to stop the demonstrators breaking through. Police using riot shields, batons and dogs kept the protesters out and there were casualties on both sides.

The violent protests gained a lot of publicity in the media. Make Poverty History campaigners criticised the violence and claimed it had nothing to do with the message they were trying to get across. First Minister, Jack McConnell, said the violence and property damage would not help the poorest countries in Africa.

Groups such as Dissent, the Wombles and the Clandestine Insurgent Rebel Clown Army, felt they were successful in forcing the leaders of rich countries to listen. They urged the public to continue other forms of direct action such as boycotting products to put pressure on the rich countries.

Question 1 (c) (continued)

SOURCE 3

Result of Survey on Involvement in Forms of Political Action

Level of participation in activity	Survey Question: Over the past twelve months, have you taken part in any of the following actions to influence rules, laws or policies?	
	Form of Action	**Percentage answering yes**
Less active participation ↕ **More active participation**	Donated money to an organisation	67%
	Signed a petition	50%
	Bought certain products as part of a campaign	39%
	Raised funds for an organisation	32%
	Worn or displayed a campaign badge or sticker	28%
	Attended a political meeting or rally	7%
	Taken part in a public demonstration	6%
	Boycotted certain products	41%
	Contacted the media	11%
	Participated in illegal protest activities	2%

Pressure Groups can only achieve their aims if they use direct action and illegal methods.

View of Bob Ure

Using Sources 1, 2 and 3 above and opposite, give **two** reasons to **support** and **two** reasons to **oppose** the view of Bob Ure.

Your answer must be based entirely on the Sources.

You must use information from each Source in your answer.

(8 marks)

[Turn over

Question 1 (continued)

(*d*) Study Sources 1, 2 and 3 below and opposite, then answer the question which follows.

SOURCE 1

Number of Constituency and Regional MSPs and Percentage (%) of MSPs by Party; Scottish Parliament Election 2003

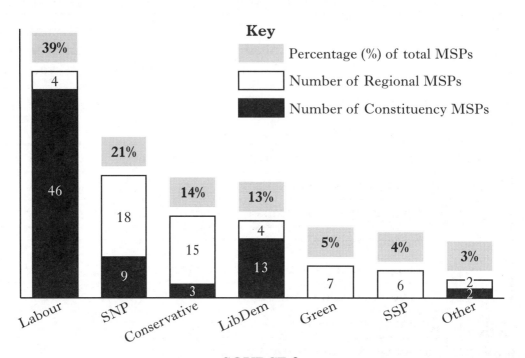

SOURCE 2

Percentage (%) of Vote by Region for the Scottish Parliament, 2003

Region	Labour	SNP	Conservative	Lib Dem	Green	SSP	Other
Central Scotland	40·4	22·5	9·2	5·9	4·7	7·2	10·1
Glasgow	38·3	17·2	7·6	7·3	7·2	15·4	7·0
Highlands and Islands	22·3	23·4	16·0	18·8	8·3	5·3	5·9
Lothians	24·5	16·2	15·1	11·0	12·0	5·4	15·7
Mid Scotland and Fife	25·3	23·0	17·6	12·0	6·9	4·6	10·6
North East Scotland	20·2	27·3	17·4	18·8	5·2	4·2	6·9
South of Scotland	30·0	18·4	24·2	10·3	5·7	5·4	6·0
West of Scotland	32·6	19·6	15·7	12·3	5·7	7·2	7·0
Scotland	29·4	20·9	15·5	11·8	6·9	6·7	8·9

Question 1 (d) (continued)

SOURCE 3

Result of Scottish Parliament Election 2003

Under the Additional Member System (AMS) used for Scottish Parliament elections, voters have two votes each. The first vote is to elect a constituency MSP using the First Past the Post system. The second vote is for a regional MSP using the Party List system. This method of voting produces a result which is fairly, but not completely, proportional in the way the parties are represented.

No party achieved an overall majority in the 2003 election because the AMS is a proportional voting system. After the 1999 election and in 2003, a coalition was formed between the Labour Party and the Liberal Democrats. Although the Labour Party was the biggest party in both elections that have been held, its support varies across the country. Even although Scotland is a fairly small country there are considerable variations in the support parties receive across the different regions.

A total of 129 MSPs are elected to the Scottish Parliament. One result of the AMS method of voting is that a wide range of parties and others are elected to the Parliament. Parties such as the Greens and the Scottish Socialist Party (SSP) are represented in the Scottish Parliament although they have no representatives in the UK Parliament.

Using Sources 1, 2 and 3 above and opposite, what **conclusions** can be drawn about the result of the Scottish Parliament Election in 2003?

You should reach conclusions about at least **three** of the following:

- success of different parties in the election

- formation of the Scottish Executive

- fairness of the Additional Member System of voting

- differences across the regions of Scotland.

You must use information from all the Sources. You should compare information within and between the Sources.

(8 marks)

NOW GO TO SECTION B ON PAGE 15

[BLANK PAGE]

STUDY THEME 1B: GOVERNMENT AND DECISION MAKING IN CENTRAL GOVERNMENT

Question 2

(*a*)

> MPs can represent their constituents in the House of Commons in a number of ways.

Describe, **in detail**, **two** ways MPs can represent their constituents in the House of Commons.

(4 marks)

(*b*)

> The UK Government is usually a majority government, made up of only one political party.

Explain, **in detail**, why some people believe a majority government, made up of only one political party, is a good way of governing the UK.

(6 marks)

[Turn over

Question 2 (continued)

(c) Study Sources 1, 2 and 3 below and opposite, then answer the question which follows.

SOURCE 1

General Election 2005 Factfile

- On 5 May 2005, Labour won 355 seats, 47 fewer than in 2001. This was a majority of 65 over all the other parties combined. The Conservatives won 197 seats; an increase of 33, and the Liberal Democrats won 62, an increase of 11.

- Labour gained 35·2% of the vote, the lowest share ever by a winning party at a UK General Election and 5·5% less than in 2001.

- Turnout in the election was 60·6% in Scotland and 61·3% in the UK as a whole.

- It is common during a General Election for newspapers to sell more copies during the campaign as voters wish to find out more about the issues.

- News broadcasts on television report higher viewing figures during the weeks before election day.

- In a survey of electors, it was reported that most had a greater trust in what was reported about politics on television compared with newspaper coverage.

- Many voters felt that there was too much coverage of politics in the media.

SOURCE 2

Survey of Newspaper Readers in Scotland

	Percentage (%) of readers who believe voting is a responsibility	Percentage (%) of readers who voted in the last General Election
Herald	89%	87%
Scotsman	95%	89%
Express/Mail	82%	82%
Record/Mirror	69%	71%
Sun	59%	55%
Does not read newspaper	59%	57%

Question 2 (c) (continued)

SOURCE 3

Adapted extracts from selected newspapers in Scotland during the 2005 General Election

The Scotsman

Labour should be returned to power, but with a sharply reduced majority . . .
To achieve this result, voters should consider tactical voting to punish Labour in its marginal constituencies. In particular, voters should favour independent-minded individuals capable of criticising not only the Government but also their own party leaders.

The Scottish Daily Mail

Conservative leader, Mr Howard, has shown enormous stamina and courage in reviving his party. The Conservatives may still seem something of a one-man band but at least they offer the hope of restoring honesty to public life and introducing sensible policies on Europe and the economy. It is because we believe these reforms are vital to the future of Britain that this paper supports the Conservatives.

The Herald

Today, the Prime Minister deserves to be punished at the polls for Iraq. Ideally, Labour will be returned to power with a much-reduced majority that causes Mr Blair to leave office much earlier than planned. The country needs a strong opposition criticising the Government from a position of strength.

The Sunday Mail

This General Election is not just a vote on Iraq, a war we are still 100 per cent against. It is a simple choice between a Labour or a Conservative Government . . . Labour is the only party capable of making Britain a fair and prosperous country . . .

Newspapers play an important part in elections in Britain.

View of Jane Ross

Using Sources 1, 2 and 3 above and opposite, give **two** reasons to **support** and **two** reasons to **oppose** the view of Jane Ross.

Your answer must be based entirely on the Sources.

You must use information from each Source in your answer.

(8 marks)

[Turn over

Question 2 (continued)

(d) Study Sources 1, 2 and 3 below and opposite, then answer the question which follows.

SOURCE 1

2005 General Election: percentage (%) turnout by age group and area

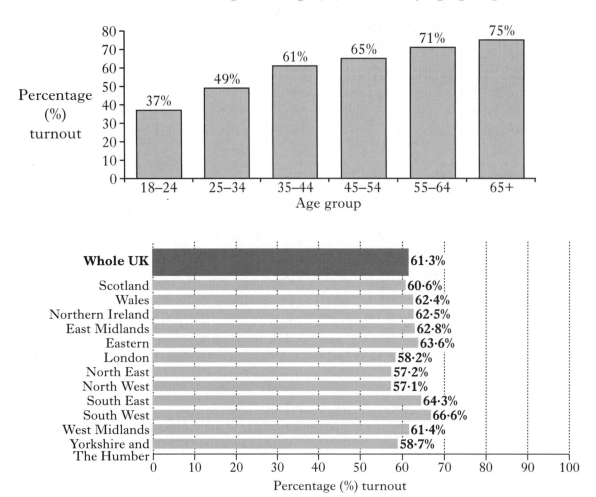

SOURCE 2

Turnout in Parliament and Council Elections

Election	Year	Turnout %
UK General Election	2005	61·5%
UK General Election	2001	59·4%
Scottish Parliament Election	2003	49·4%
Scottish Parliament Election	1999	59·1%
European Parliament Election	2004	38·4%
European Parliament Election	1999	24·0%
English Local Council Elections	2004	40·1%
Scottish Local Council Elections	2003	49·2%
Welsh Local Council Elections	2004	43·2%
Northern Ireland Local Council Elections	2001	66·0%

Question 2 (*d*) (continued)

SOURCE 3

Election Turnout in the United Kingdom

Turnout has varied considerably in elections in the UK. The highest turnout for a general election in the UK was 83·9% in 1950. Since that date, election turnout has never been as high. The lowest point in general election turnout came in 2001, although it rose again in 2005. From the 1960s to the 1990s, turnout in UK general elections was always above 70%.

One factor which seems to have an effect upon turnout is how powerful and important is the parliament or council being elected. If voters see the result of the election having a big effect upon their lives, they will be more likely to vote. If the parliament or council is not seen as being so important then they will be less likely to vote. Younger voters seem to be less interested in voting than those in older age groups.

Where you live seems to have an effect upon whether or not people vote. In some parts of the country, there are many safe seats; in others there are more marginal seats. Voters are more likely to vote in those areas where the result is close so their vote may have more effect on the overall result.

Using Sources 1, 2 and 3 above and opposite, what **conclusions** can be drawn about turnout in elections in Britain?

You should reach conclusions about at least **three** of the following:

- changes over time

- age of voters

- the parliament or council being elected

- area of the UK.

You must use information from all the Sources. You should compare information within and between the Sources.

(8 marks)

NOW GO TO SECTION B ON PAGE 15

[BLANK PAGE]

SECTION B – SOCIAL ISSUES IN THE UNITED KINGDOM

Answer **ONE** question only:

Question 3 Study Theme 2A – Equality in Society: Wealth and Health in the
United Kingdom   on pages 15–17
OR Question 4 Study Theme 2B – Crime and the Law in Society on pages 19–21

STUDY THEME 2A: EQUALITY IN SOCIETY: WEALTH AND HEALTH IN THE UNITED KINGDOM

Question 3

(*a*) | The National Health Service in Scotland provides both primary and secondary health care services.

Describe, **in detail**, primary and secondary health care services provided by the NHS in Scotland.

(6 marks)

(*b*) | Reducing poverty in the United Kingdom is an important government policy.

Explain, **in detail**, why reducing poverty in the United Kingdom is an important government policy.

(8 marks)

[Turn over

Question 3 (continued)

(c) Study Sources 1, 2 and 3 below and opposite, then answer the question which follows.

You are an adviser to the Scottish Executive. You have been asked to recommend whether or not to abolish prescription charges.

Option 1	**Option 2**
Abolish prescription charges.	Do not abolish prescription charges.

SOURCE 1

Facts and Viewpoints

- In Scotland, 1 in 4 children (280 000) live in poor households. Children are affected when parents face ill-health and cannot afford their own prescriptions.
- The Scottish NHS Confederation claims that the lost income will be equal to losing 175 full-time nurses.
- Welfare to work policies move people into work but the loss of benefits, such as free prescriptions, leaves them only slightly better off.
- The income raised from prescription charges amounted to £46·3 million in 2002–2003.
- The NHS prescription drugs bill has increased every year.
- The prescription charge in 2006 was £6·65 per item.
- Some long-term medical conditions are exempt from charges while others are not.
- 80% of people aged between 18 and 60 are required to pay for prescriptions.
- The current system disadvantages a significant proportion, as many children living below the official poverty line live in working households with household incomes above £14 600, above which adults must pay for their prescriptions.
- Around 50% of the population does not have to pay for prescriptions and around 92% of items dispensed are provided free of charge.

SOURCE 2

Attitude of Health Related Organisations to the Abolition of Prescription Charges

	For Abolition	Unclear	Against Abolition
Asthma UK Ltd	✓		
Citizens Advice Scotland	✓		
Guild of Health Care		✓	
NHS Grampian			✓
NHS Lanarkshire			✓
NHS Tayside		✓	
Royal College of Physicians and Surgeons			✓
Royal Pharmaceutical Society	✓		
Scottish Association for Mental Health	✓		
Scottish NHS Confederation			✓

Question 3 (c) (continued)

SOURCE 2 (continued)

**Total Cost of Prescriptions
Amount paid by Patient and Amount paid by NHS, 1996–2004**

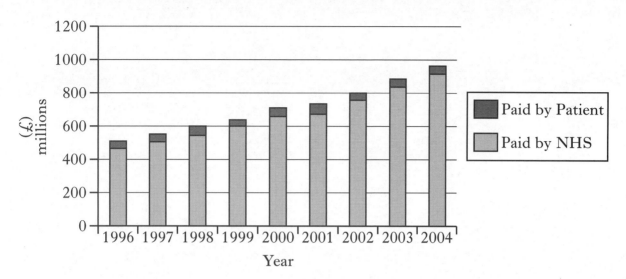

SOURCE 3

Viewpoints

Prescription charges should be abolished. Although children and many of our poorest adults do not have to pay for prescriptions, many low-income families are still unable to afford prescribed medicine. Abolishing prescription charges will help to reduce health inequalities associated with poverty. The poorest families would have more money to spend, allowing diet and living conditions to improve. Far from earning the NHS extra income, prescription charges could end up costing the NHS much more in expensive hospital treatment. Eight out of ten doctors reported that patients were missing out on necessary drugs because they could not afford them.

Local Poverty Action Group Spokesperson

Prescription charges should not be abolished. One of the aims of prescription charging was to limit demand for treatment by putting a price on it. People will demand drugs that they do not need or which are ineffective in treating their condition, for example, antibiotics for colds. The government already pays most of the cost of each prescription item. More money is going to have to be put into health care and the NHS needs every penny it can get.

Political Party Spokesperson

You must decide which option to recommend to the Scottish Executive, **either** to abolish prescription charges **or** not to abolish prescription charges.

Using Sources 1, 2 and 3 above and opposite, **which option would you choose**?

Give reasons to **support** your choice.

Explain why you did not make the other choice.

Your answer must be based on all the Sources.

(10 marks)

NOW GO TO SECTION C ON PAGE 23

[BLANK PAGE]

STUDY THEME 2B: CRIME AND THE LAW IN SOCIETY

Question 4

(*a*) | Changes have been made to laws in Scotland on smoking and alcohol in recent years. |

Describe, **in detail**, the changes that have been made to laws in Scotland on smoking and alcohol in recent years.

(6 marks)

(*b*) | There are many reasons why some people commit crime. |

Explain, **in detail**, why some people commit crime.

(8 marks)

[Turn over

Question 4 (continued)

(c) Study Sources 1, 2 and 3 below and opposite, then answer the question which follows.

You are an adviser to the UK Government. You have been asked to recommend whether or not the police should be given additional powers to detain terrorist suspects for up to 90 days without charge.

Option 1	Option 2
Give police additional powers to detain terrorist suspects for up to 90 days without charge.	Do not give police additional powers to detain terrorist suspects for up to 90 days without charge.

SOURCE 1

Selected Facts and Viewpoints

- Detention for 90 days is against civil liberties.
- Since the attack on the USA on September 11 2001, Britain has also been a target for terrorists.
- The increased threat from international terrorism means that the police need increased powers.
- To increase maximum detention to 90 days would be against the UK's international human rights responsibilities.
- The complexity of a terrorist investigation means that police need more time to investigate before charges are brought.
- Imprisonment without charge for 90 days will do more harm than good and lead to resentment and more recruits to terrorism.
- Supporters argue that the police need the extra time because of the difficulties of gathering evidence from overseas and from coded computer messages.
- The rights of those detained would be protected because a judge would need to approve the continuing detention at regular intervals throughout the 90 days.
- The increased powers could lead to a worsening of community and race relations in the UK.

SOURCE 2
Arrests in the UK under the Terrorism Act 2000, September 2001 to September 2005

Convicted of offences under the Terrorism Act	23
Charged under the Terrorism Act	115
Charged under other legislation	156
Transferred to Immigration authorities	63
Released without charge	496
Other outcomes	42
Total arrests	**895**

Question 4 (c) (continued)

SOURCE 2 (continued)

Results of a YouGov Poll
Question
Do you think it may sometimes be necessary to restrict the civil liberties of suspected terrorists even though there is not enough evidence to charge and convict them?

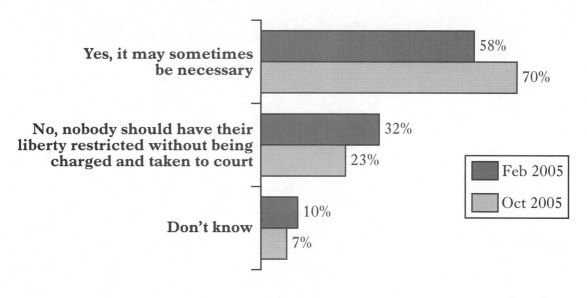

SOURCE 3

Viewpoints

The police should be given powers to detain terrorist suspects for up to 90 days due to the recent increase in the threat of terrorism. It would only be in a very few cases where a person would have to be detained for the full 90 days. More time is needed to gather evidence against suspects because of the nature of attacks like the 2005 London bombings. The investigations into the events of July 2005 produced 80 000 videos of CCTV footage and 1400 sets of fingerprints at 160 suspected crime scenes.

Police Spokesperson

The police should not be given powers to detain terrorist suspects for up to 90 days; the current 28-day rule is sufficient. It is just as bad as detention without trial. The Law Lords have ruled that detention without trial is illegal and unacceptable. It seriously undermines the right to a fair trial, and the principle that you are innocent until proven guilty. This country is in danger of abandoning its democratic values.

Human Rights Spokesperson

You must decide which option to recommend to the UK Government, **either** to give the police additional powers **or** not to give the police additional powers to detain terrorist suspects for up to 90 days without charge.

Using Sources 1, 2 and 3 above and opposite, **which option would you choose**?

Give reasons to **support** your choice.

Explain why you did not make the other choice.

Your answer must be based on all the Sources.

(10 marks)

NOW GO TO SECTION C ON PAGE 23

[BLANK PAGE]

SECTION C – INTERNATIONAL ISSUES

Answer **ONE** question only:

       Question 5 Study Theme 3A – The Republic of South Africa on pages 23–25
OR Question 6 Study Theme 3B – The People's Republic of China on pages 26–27
OR Question 7 Study Theme 3C – The United States of America on pages 28–29
OR Question 8 Study Theme 3D – The European Union on pages 30–31
OR Question 9 Study Theme 3E – Development in Brazil on pages 32–33

STUDY THEME 3A: THE REPUBLIC OF SOUTH AFRICA

Question 5

(*a*) | Many non-white South Africans have made economic progress in recent years. |

Describe, **in detail**, the economic progress made by many non-white South Africans in recent years.

(6 marks)

(*b*) | The Government of South Africa faces political opposition from various groups. |

Explain, **in detail**, why the Government of South Africa faces political opposition from various groups.

(6 marks)

[Turn over

Question 5 (continued)

(c)   Study Sources 1, 2 and 3 below and opposite, then answer the question which follows.

SOURCE 1

Percentage (%) of adults with HIV/AIDS in selected African Countries, 2001 and 2003

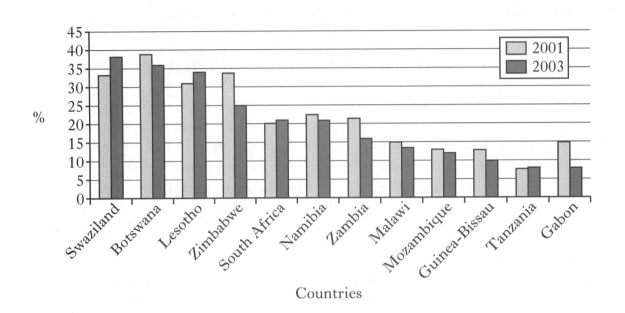

Countries

SOURCE 2

Percentage (%) of people with HIV attending antenatal clinics by Province

Province	2002	2003	2004
KwaZulu Natal	36·5%	37·5%	40·7%
Gauteng	31·6%	29·6%	33·1%
Mpumalanga	28·6%	32·6%	30·8%
Free State	28·8%	30·1%	29·5%
Eastern Cape	23·6%	27·1%	28·0%
North West	26·2%	29·9%	26·7%
Limpopo	15·6%	17·5%	19·3%
Northern Cape	15·1%	16·7%	17·6%
Western Cape	12·4%	13·1%	15·4%
South Africa	**26·5%**	**27·9%**	**29·5%**

Question 5 (c) (continued)

SOURCE 3

Massive Resources to Combat AIDS

The Government of South Africa is massively increasing resources in the fight against HIV/AIDS, with plans to spend more than 3 billion Rand over the next 3 years on anti-retroviral drugs. These drugs can prevent the transmission of the HIV virus to unborn babies. According to a recent survey between 5 and 6 million South Africans were HIV positive. This includes 3·1 million women and 2·4 million men between the ages of 15 and 49. An estimated 96 228 babies were infected.

Funding to assist the management, care and treatment of HIV/AIDS has also increased and there is evidence that the disease is on the decline in some provinces although it has not declined nationally. Despite the health budget increase of 11·4%, to a total of 9·5 billion Rand in 2005, challenges remain. There is still a shortage of medically trained staff in many parts of the country. Also, the anti-retroviral drug, Nevirapine, is still not reaching enough pregnant mothers who have HIV. This is due mainly to a lack of health care services, particularly in rural areas.

In response to criticisms, the Government has said there will be extra funding available. The provinces of KwaZulu Natal, Western Cape and Gauteng claim that they now provide almost complete access to Nevirapine and other provinces say they are making steady progress. A spokesperson for the Government also claims that the problem of HIV/AIDS in South Africa is not as bad as in other African countries.

The South African Government has been successful in dealing with HIV/AIDS in recent years.

View of Health Minister

Using Sources 1, 2 and 3, explain why the Health Minister is being **selective in the use of facts**.

Your answer must be based entirely on the Sources above and opposite.

(8 marks)

NOW CHECK THAT YOU HAVE ANSWERED ONE QUESTION FROM EACH OF SECTIONS A, B AND C

STUDY THEME 3B: THE PEOPLE'S REPUBLIC OF CHINA

Question 6

(*a*)

There are opportunities for political participation and representation in China.

Describe, **in detail**, the opportunities for political participation and representation in China.

(6 marks)

(*b*)

People in some parts of China have better living standards than those in other areas.

Explain, **in detail**, why people in some parts of China have better living standards than those in other areas.

(6 marks)

(*c*)   Study Sources 1, 2 and 3 below and opposite, then answer the question which follows.

SOURCE 1

Deaths in the Workplace in China

Total Number of Deaths in the Workplace		Number of Deaths in Selected Occupations in 2003	
Year	**Deaths**		
2000	8634	Coal mining	4620
2001	9562	Other mining	1626
2002	10 305	Non-mining industries	5203
2003	11 449		
2004	11 394		

Question 6 (c) (continued)

SOURCE 2
Number of Industrial Accidents in Selected Countries, 2003 and 2004

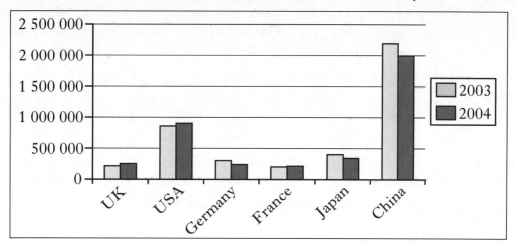

SOURCE 3

Accidents at work in China

Industrial accidents in China are among the highest in the world. However, the death toll in workplace accidents which had been rising until 2003 has begun to fall. Some workers blame the unacceptably high number of accidents on China's rush towards more production. Workers are working longer hours since state owned industries were privatised. Health and safety is a low priority.

Deaths in the coal industry dropped by 25% even though total coal output increased by 19%. Extremely serious accidents, those with more than 30 people killed, also showed a decline. However, in chemical production, the situation is not so good. Outdated technology, ageing facilities and poor management have combined to increase the number of accidents in that industry. In April 2004, chemical accidents resulted in 23 deaths, 300 people being poisoned and the evacuation of 150 000 people in Guangdong Province.

The Chinese Government has responded to accidents at work by stating that new technology should be used to improve safety and rescue operations whenever there is a serious accident. Emergency rescue operations should be developed to ensure that professional quick response rescue teams are well prepared. In defending its record, the Chinese authorities point out that there are more accidents in China as its population is approximately four times the size of the USA.

China has a good record regarding accidents in the workplace.

View of Chinese Government Official

Using Sources 1, 2 and 3, explain why the Chinese Government Official is being **selective in the use of facts**.

Your answer must be based entirely on the Sources above and opposite.

(8 marks)

NOW CHECK THAT YOU HAVE ANSWERED ONE QUESTION FROM EACH OF SECTIONS A, B AND C

STUDY THEME 3C: THE UNITED STATES OF AMERICA

Question 7

(*a*) | American citizens have many opportunities to take part in the political system. |

Describe, **in detail**, ways in which American citizens can take part in the political system.

(6 marks)

(*b*) | Some ethnic groups in the USA do better in employment than others. |

Explain, **in detail**, why some ethnic groups in the USA do better in employment than others.

(6 marks)

(*c*) Study Sources 1, 2 and 3 below and opposite, then answer the question which follows.

SOURCE 1

Health Insurance Factfile

The USA spends huge amounts of money on health care. The health care costs of most Americans are met by private health insurance that they pay for themselves or is provided by their employers. There are two government schemes for elderly and poor Americans – Medicare and Medicaid. Large numbers of Americans, however, have no health care insurance at all and must pay their own medical bills if they become ill. In 2003, 245 million people in the USA had health insurance coverage – 84·4% of the population. An estimated 15·6% of the population, or 45 million people, were without any health insurance coverage, an increase from 15·2% in 2002.

The percentage of Black Americans without insurance did not change. It was 20% and for Asian Americans about 19%. The percentage of Whites without health insurance increased from 10·7% to 11·1%. The uninsured rate for Hispanics was 33% in 2003 – the same figure as in 2002. The actual number of Hispanics without health insurance increased from 12·8 million to 13·2 million due to population growth. The percentage of American Indian and Alaskan Native who were without medical insurance cover was 27·5%.

Of the 245 million Americans with some form of health insurance coverage in 2003, 60·4% were covered by employment-based and private schemes. The percentage of people covered by government health insurance programmes such as Medicaid and Medicare rose from 25·7% to 26·6%.

Question 7 (*c*) (continued)

SOURCE 2

Life Expectancy (in years) by Ethnic Origin and Gender

	Male	Female
Total Population	74·1	79·8
White	74·7	80·1
Black	68·4	75·1
American Indian and Alaskan Native	72·9	82·0
Asian	80·9	86·5
Hispanic	77·2	83·7

SOURCE 3

Infant Mortality Rate

Infant deaths per 1000 live births

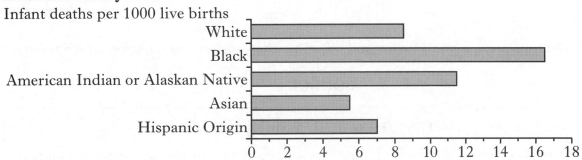

Breast Cancer Rate

Deaths per 100 000 women

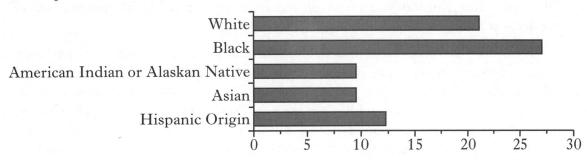

Compared to White Americans, all ethnic minorities in the USA suffer poorer health and have less access to health care.

View of an American Doctor

Using Sources 1, 2 and 3, explain why the American Doctor is being **selective in the use of facts**.

Your answer must be based entirely on the Sources above and opposite.

(8 marks)

NOW CHECK THAT YOU HAVE ANSWERED ONE QUESTION FROM EACH OF SECTIONS A, B AND C

STUDY THEME 3D: THE EUROPEAN UNION

Question 8

(a) | Aid is available to help poorer parts of the European Union (EU). |

Describe, **in detail**, the aid that is available to help poorer parts of the European Union (EU).

(6 marks)

(b) | Some people are against further enlargement of the European Union (EU). |

Explain, **in detail**, why some people are against further enlargement of the European Union (EU).

(6 marks)

(c) Study Sources 1, 2 and 3 below and opposite, then answer the question which follows.

SOURCE 1

The Effects of EU Fishing Policy

The Commission of the European Union has set new maximum fishing catches (quotas), which all member states have to abide by. It is hoped that this will have the effect of allowing fish stocks to grow in the future. The problem is that ever growing demand for fish has meant that there are less fish in the seas and the fish which are there are too small. Obviously, this will have an effect on the fishing industry in all member states but these effects will not be shared equally.

Britain's fishing fleet has been in serious decline for many years. Around 50 years ago, the industry employed more than 30 000 people but today the figure is much less. Among the hardest hit areas has been Scotland's East coast in places such as Fraserburgh and Peterhead where white fish such as cod and haddock are relied upon. Critics claim that EU quotas are not fair and some fish have not been included in the ban. French and Spanish fishermen will continue to be allowed to fish for monkfish, sole and prawns off their coastlines. This means that they will continue to make a good living.

In contrast, the fish processing industry has been booming in recent years. In places such as Grimsby on England's East coast, there are several firms which, together, process just under 1 million tonnes of fish per year. That figure is almost five times the UK's EU fishing quota. Much of the fish comes from Iceland and the Faroe Islands which are not involved in the EU fish quota system. The UK economy benefits from fish processing which involves freezing the fish in order to keep it fresh. More and more jobs are being created as this industry expands.

Page thirty

Question 8 (*c*) (continued)

SOURCE 2

Number of people employed in the UK Fishing Industry (1985–2005)

Number of Fishermen employed in selected EU countries (2005)

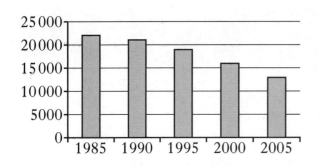
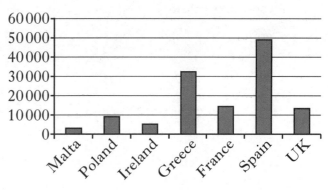

SOURCE 3

Factfile on Fishing Industry in the UK and Selected EU Member States

- Spain earns more from fishing than any other EU country.

- 60% of jobs in Fraserburgh and Peterhead, Scotland's main fishing areas, are directly linked to "white" fishing.

- Peterhead's fishing fleet has declined by 60% since the 1970s.

- Stocks of haddock and cod have begun to recover in the North Sea off the Scottish coast.

- Average crew earnings by UK fishermen on British boats fell from £23 000 in 2002 to £13 000 in 2004.

- £540 million worth of fish caught in 2002 were worth a total of £1 billion to the UK economy after processing.

- The fishing industry warns that more limits on fishing will result in a loss of jobs in fish processing and this could greatly harm the UK economy.

The fishing industry in the UK continues to improve and compete with the rest of the European Union (EU).

View of Scottish Fisheries Spokesperson

Using Sources 1, 2 and 3, explain why the Scottish Fisheries Spokesperson is being **selective in the use of facts**.

Your answer must be based entirely on the Sources above and opposite.

(8 marks)

NOW CHECK THAT YOU HAVE ANSWERED ONE QUESTION FROM EACH OF SECTIONS A, B AND C.

STUDY THEME 3E: DEVELOPMENT IN BRAZIL

Question 9

(*a*)

> Some groups in Brazil have made progress in recent years.

Describe, **in detail**, the progress made by some groups in Brazil in recent years.

(6 marks)

(*b*)

> The Government of Brazil faces political opposition.

Explain, **in detail**, the reasons why the Government of Brazil faces political opposition.

(6 marks)

(*c*)　Study Sources 1, 2 and 3 below and opposite, then answer the question which follows.

SOURCE 1

Prisons in Brazil

Brazil does not have a national prison system. All prisons are run by the different states, so there are 27 prison systems. However, there is one single prison law for the whole country. This says clearly how prisons should be run and the rights and duties of the prisoners. Despite this, the rights of prisoners in many prisons in Brazil are ignored. Many prisons have high levels of overcrowding and violence and corruption are widespread. The levels of overcrowding are so bad that in one police station in Rio de Janeiro, 65 prisoners were held in a cell measuring 12 square metres.

Action has been taken to address the problem of overcrowding in prisons. From 1995 to 2003, great efforts were made to build new prisons. Dozens of new prisons were built throughout the country. Efforts have also been made to reduce the number of people going to prison in some states. Some states in Brazil are beginning to look at alternatives to prison for some people convicted of a crime, such as community service, in order to tackle the overcrowding problem.

Youth Detention Centres have also had problems with overcrowding. In some centres, youths often share beds or sleep on the floor. Cells are filthy, dark and infested with rats. At times, youths wear the same clothes for a week. Youths do not always have access to soap and toothpaste. Some cities, such as Rio de Janeiro, have made attempts to improve the conditions in their youth detention centres and reduce the level of overcrowding.

Question 9 (c) (continued)

SOURCE 2

Brazil: Prison Population, Capacity and Overcrowding (1995 to 2003)

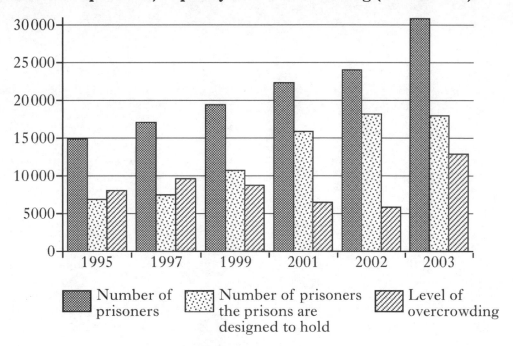

SOURCE 3

Youth Detention Centres – Rio de Janeiro (2005)

Name of Detention Centre	Number of Youths in Detention	Level of Overcrowding
CAI-Baixada	120	95
CTR	37	0
Joao Luiz Alves	108	0
Padre Severino	160	98
Santo Expedito	166	35
Santos Dumont	36	0

> Progress has been made to reduce overcrowding in prisons and youth detention centres in Brazil.

View of Government Official

Using Sources 1, 2 and 3, explain why the Government Official is being **selective in the use of facts**.

Your answer must be based entirely on the Sources above and opposite.

(8 marks)

NOW CHECK THAT YOU HAVE ANSWERED ONE QUESTION FROM EACH OF SECTIONS A, B AND C

[END OF QUESTION PAPER]

[BLANK PAGE]

[BLANK PAGE]

X236/201

NATIONAL
QUALIFICATIONS
2008

THURSDAY, 29 MAY
9.00 AM – 11.00 AM

MODERN STUDIES
INTERMEDIATE 2

This Examination Paper consists of 3 Sections. Within each Section there is a choice of Study Themes. There is one question for each Study Theme.

Section A – Political Issues in the United Kingdom (answer one question)
Question 1 Study Theme 1A Government and Decision Making in Scotland   Pages 2 – 3
Question 2 Study Theme 1B Government and Decision Making in Central Government Pages 4 – 5

Section B – Social Issues in the United Kingdom (answer one question)
Question 3 Study Theme 2A Equality in Society: Wealth and Health in the United Kingdom

                                                                                Pages 7 – 9
Question 4 Study Theme 2B Crime and the Law in Society   Pages 11 – 13

Section C – International Issues (answer one question)
Question 5 Study Theme 3A The Republic of South Africa   Pages 15 –19
Question 6 Study Theme 3B The People's Republic of China   Pages 21 – 25
Question 7 Study Theme 3C The United States of America   Pages 27 – 31
Question 8 Study Theme 3D The European Union   Pages 33 – 37
Question 9 Study Theme 3E Development in Brazil   Pages 39 – 43

Total Marks – 70

1   Read the questions carefully.

2   You must answer **one** question from **each** of Section A, Section B and Section C.

3   You must answer **all** parts of the questions you choose. Questions in Sections A and B each have three parts; Questions in Section C each have four parts.

4   You should spend approximately 40 minutes on each Section.

5   If you cannot do a question or part of a question, move on and try again later.

6   Write your answers in the book provided. Indicate clearly, in the left hand margin, the question and section of question being answered. Do not write in the right hand margin.

SECTION A – POLITICAL ISSUES IN THE UNITED KINGDOM

Answer **ONE** question only:

> Question 1   Study Theme 1A – Government and Decision Making in Scotland
> on pages 2 and 3
> **OR**   Question 2   Study Theme 1B – Government and Decision Making in Central Government
> on pages 4 and 5

STUDY THEME 1A: GOVERNMENT AND DECISION MAKING IN SCOTLAND

Question 1

(*a*)

> Local councils are responsible for providing services in their own area.

Describe, **in detail**, services local councils are responsible for providing in their own area.

(6 marks)

(*b*)

> Pressure groups use campaigning methods which will attract the attention of the media.

Explain, **in detail**, why pressure groups use campaigning methods which will attract the attention of the media.

(6 marks)

(*c*)   Study Sources 1, 2 and 3 below and on *Page three*, then answer the question which follows.

SOURCE 1

Scotland Profile 2007

Gender and Racial Profile of Scotland	
Male	49%
Female	51%
White	98%
Ethnic Minority	2%

Scottish Parliament Election 2007	
Party	Percentage (%) Share of Vote
Scottish National Party	32·0%
Labour	30·6%
Conservative	15·2%
Liberal Democrat	13·7%
Green	2·1%
Others	6·4%

Question 1 (*c*) (continued)

SOURCE 2

Minority Government Formed

The voting system used to elect the Scottish Parliament is known as the Additional Member System. It is a system of voting which usually produces a fairly proportional result. The election was held on 3 May 2007. After several days of discussions, no agreement was reached between the Scottish National Party and any of the larger parties to form a coalition government. A minority SNP Government was formed with the backing of the Green Party to begin to carry out the devolved powers of the Parliament.

There was a fall in the number of women elected to the Scottish Parliament — 43 women were elected, a third of the total. This is still one of the highest figures in the world. The first ethnic minority MSP was elected to the Scottish Parliament.

The SNP minority Government aims to use its devolved powers, tackling problems in education and health. Some of their first actions were abolishing tolls on the Tay and Forth Road bridges, scrapping the student endowment and introducing a ban on under 18 year olds buying cigarettes. However, the new Government will not find it easy to carry out all its policies. Since all the other parties can out-vote the SNP Government it must be careful to seek agreement from its political rivals. The SNP will face a delay in putting forward its policy of a referendum on independence for Scotland.

SOURCE 3

Composition of the Scottish Parliament

Party	Number of MSPs	Percentage (%) of MSPs	Government/Opposition
Scottish National Party	47	36·4%	Minority Government (47 MSPs)
Labour	46	35·6%	Opposition Parties (82 MSPs)
Conservative	17	13·2%	
Liberal Democrat	16	12·4%	
Scottish Green Party	2	1·6%	
Independent	1	0·8%	
Total	129	100%	

The Scottish Parliament is effective both in representing the people of Scotland and in carrying out its devolved powers.

View of Nazia Issa

Using Sources 1, 2 and 3, explain why Nazia Issa is being **selective in the use of facts**.

Your answer must be based entirely on the Sources above and opposite.

You must use information from each Source in your answer.

(8 marks)

NOW GO TO SECTION B ON PAGE 7

STUDY THEME 1B: GOVERNMENT AND DECISION MAKING IN CENTRAL GOVERNMENT

Question 2

(a)

> Newspapers play an important role in politics.

Describe, **in detail**, ways in which newspapers play a role in politics.

(6 marks)

(b)

> Some people choose not to vote in elections.

Explain, **in detail**, why some people choose not to vote in elections.

(6 marks)

(c) Study Sources 1, 2 and 3 below and on *Page five*, then answer the question which follows.

SOURCE 1

United Kingdom Profile 2005

Gender and Racial Profile of the United Kingdom	
Male	49·0%
Female	51·0%
White	92·0%
Ethnic Minority	8·0%

UK Parliament Election 2005	
Parties in the House of Commons	Percentage (%) Share of Vote
Labour	35·2%
Conservative	32·3%
Liberal Democrat	22·1%
Scottish National Party	1·4%
Others	9·0%

SOURCE 2

Clear Victory for Labour Government

The voting system used to elect the House of Commons is known as First Past the Post. It is a straightforward system which usually produces a clear result quickly. The election was held on Thursday 5 May 2005. By the early hours of Friday morning, it was clear that Labour had won a third term of office. On the day after the election, the leader of the Labour Party was summoned by the Queen and asked to form a government. Later that same day the Prime Minister was choosing his senior ministers to govern the country.

A record number of women were elected — 128 women were elected to the House of Commons, almost 20% of the total. Fifteen ethnic minority MPs were elected. This was also the highest figure ever elected, at just over 2% of MPs.

The Government aims to govern the country, tackling problems in education and health, introducing new laws to improve security, reduce crime and deal with issues overseas. However, the Government has not always found it easy to govern. It has faced criticism from the opposition parties and on certain policies it has not received support from some members of its own party. Some Labour MPs have voted against their own party on issues such as the detention of terrorist suspects and the conduct of the war in Iraq.

SOURCE 3

Composition of the House of Commons

Party	Number of MPs	Percentage (%) of MPs	Government/Opposition
Labour	356	55·1%	Government Party (356 MPs)
Conservative	197	30·5%	Opposition Parties (290 MPs)
Liberal Democrats	62	9·6%	
Scottish National Party	6	0·9%	
Others	25	3·9%	
Total	646	100%	

The House of Commons is effective both in representing the people of Britain and in governing the country.

View of Lucy Tang

Using Sources 1, 2 and 3, explain why Lucy Tang is being **selective in the use of facts**.

Your answer must be based entirely on the Sources above and opposite.

You must use information from each Source in your answer.

(8 marks)

NOW GO TO SECTION B ON PAGE 7

[BLANK PAGE]

SECTION B – SOCIAL ISSUES IN THE UNITED KINGDOM

Answer **ONE** question only:

Question 3 Study Theme 2A – Equality in Society: Wealth and Health in the
United Kingdom   on pages 7–9
OR Question 4 Study Theme 2B – Crime and the Law in Society on pages 11–13

STUDY THEME 2A: EQUALITY IN SOCIETY: WEALTH AND HEALTH IN THE UNITED KINGDOM

Question 3

(*a*) | Poverty affects many people in the United Kingdom.

Describe, **in detail**, the ways in which poverty affects many people in the United Kingdom.

(6 marks)

(*b*) | Care in the community is better for some people while residential care is better for others.

Explain, **in detail**, why community care is better for some people and residential care is better for others.

(8 marks)

[Turn over

Question 3 (continued)

(*c*)   Study Sources 1, 2 and 3 below and opposite, then answer the question which follows.

You are an adviser to the Scottish Government. You have been asked to recommend whether or not to continue with the Educational Maintenance Allowance (EMA).

Option 1	**Option 2**
Continue with the Educational Maintenance Allowance (EMA).	Do not continue with the Educational Maintenance Allowance (EMA).

SOURCE 1

Selected Facts and Viewpoints

Educational Maintenance Allowance (EMA) is a payment made to some young people from low income families if they stay on at school into S5 and S6. It has been in operation across the whole of Scotland since 2004. The rates paid range from £10 to £30 per week depending on income. The EMA was introduced to reduce the number of young people not in Employment, Education or Training (NEET).

* School students not entitled to EMA often have to get a job which takes time away from their studies.

* Research has shown that staying on at school into S5 and S6 reduces the time many young people spend out of work and on benefits.

* The £20 million that EMA costs could be better spent on more teachers and textbooks.

* Before EMA, many young people from disadvantaged families left school at the earliest opportunity.

* Almost two thousand (12%) of the 16,290 students in Scotland who received the EMA between August and December 2004 did not stay on into the second half of the school year.

* The EMA will help girls as those who leave school at the earliest opportunity have less success than boys who leave early.

* Some young people spend the EMA money on luxuries or buy cigarettes and sweets.

* Young people who do not do well in S3 and S4, but stay on, do better in terms of employment in their late teens and early twenties.

SOURCE 2

Percentage (%) of 16–19 year olds not in Employment, Education or Training (NEET)

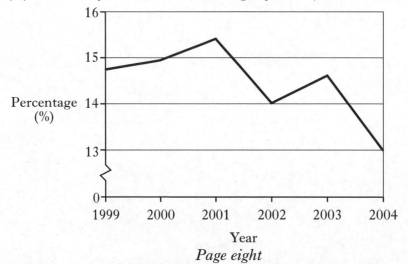

Question 3 (c) (continued)

SOURCE 2 (continued)

Percentage (%) of students who spent some of the EMA on:	
Helping with household expenses	33%
Clothes	70%
Transport costs	42%
Books or equipment for school	61%
Going out/leisure activities	63%
Paying off debts	6%
Savings	4%
Other	3%

SOURCE 3

Viewpoints

Educational Maintenance Allowance (EMA) should not continue. It is not fair. Some students in the same class receive payments while others do not. Students attend school to receive EMA but do not necessarily work hard towards gaining better qualifications. The parents of some students are able to abuse the system and get money they are not entitled to receive. Many people are staying on at school when they should leave and start working or take up a training course to deal with the skills gap that exists in Britain. Most of the money paid in EMA is spent on luxuries and extras, not on essential expenditure to keep people at school.

View of Eun Chung

Educational Maintenance Allowance (EMA) should continue. It has been a great success. EMA benefits teenagers from low-income households, encouraging people to stay in education past the legally required age of 16. With more students staying on at school and getting more qualifications, we will have a more skilled workforce in the future. Even with the EMA, parents earning less than £30,000 a year still struggle to support teenagers to enable them to stay in education. EMA helps young people pay for essential costs such as travel, books and equipment and relieves a great deal of stress in low income households.

View of Stuart Scott

You must decide which option to recommend to the Scottish Government, **either** to continue with the Educational Maintenance Allowance (EMA) **or** not to continue with the Educational Maintenance Allowance (EMA).

Using Sources 1, 2 and 3 above and opposite, **which option would you choose**?

Give reasons to **support** your choice.

Explain why you did not make the other choice.

Your answer must be based on all the Sources.

(10 marks)

NOW GO TO SECTION C ON PAGE 15

[BLANK PAGE]

STUDY THEME 2B: CRIME AND THE LAW IN SOCIETY

Question 4

(*a*) | Some young people commit crimes. |

Describe, **in detail**, the crimes most commonly committed by young people.

(6 marks)

(*b*) | In some areas community policing is the best way to tackle crime, while in others the use of CCTV cameras is better. |

Explain, **in detail**, why in some areas community policing is the best way to tackle crime, while in others the use of CCTV cameras is better.

(8 marks)

[Turn over

Question 4 (continued)

(c)   Study Sources 1, 2 and 3 below and opposite, then answer the question which follows.

You are an adviser to the Scottish Government. You have been asked to recommend whether or not to continue with the early release of prisoners.

Option 1	**Option 2**
Continue with the early release of prisoners.	Do not continue with the early release of prisoners.

SOURCE 1

Selected Facts and Viewpoints

The principle of early release means that prisoners can be released from prison before the full term of the sentence given by the court has been served. The prisoner may then have to spend a period of time on community service and/or be electronically tagged.

- The system of early release provides a way to encourage good behaviour of prisoners.

- Seeing a prisoner released early undermines the public's idea of justice.

- When on early release, the threat of being put back in prison helps to reduce the risk of re-offending.

- For victims, knowing that the offender has been released can cause stress and worry.

- The Scottish Government has established a new Risk Management Authority, which will more accurately assess the chance of a person re-offending.

- Families and relatives of the victims assume that the convicted person will serve the whole sentence given by the court.

- Over recent years the prison population has increased resulting in overcrowding.

- The number of criminals returned to prison after being released early has increased in the last 10 years with 12% in the last year alone.

SOURCE 2
Scottish Prison Population by Length of Sentence, 2002–2005

Length of Sentence	2002	2003	2004	2005
Less than four years	2073	2112	2157	2232
More than four years	1663	1685	1773	1821
Life	571	574	567	597

Question 4 (*c*) (continued)

SOURCE 2 (continued)

Number re-offending after early release, Scotland 1997–2006

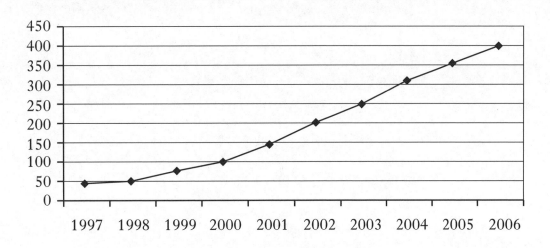

SOURCE 3

Viewpoints

The practice of early release of prisoners should continue. The law should not require every prisoner to serve the whole period of their sentence in prison. Part of the sentence, where risk of re-offending has been properly assessed, should be served in the community. Early release would reduce the strain on prisoners' families. The size of the prison population and overcrowding need to be tackled, as well as reducing the huge cost of keeping people locked up for many years. Early release should take into consideration the progress of the prisoner within the prison system.

View of Ellie Foster

The practice of early release should not continue. The law should require that every prisoner serves the whole period of imprisonment of the sentence given. Prison is a deterrent; it prevents some from committing crimes and re-offending. The public are very unhappy with the current early release system, especially when released offenders go on to re-offend. The use of electronic monitoring devices and community service is an easy option for criminals. Early release favours the prisoner not the victim. End early release and reassure the public that the offender is safely locked behind bars.

View of Eddie Wright

You must decide which option to recommend to the Scottish Government, **either** to continue with the early release of prisoners **or** not to continue with early release of prisoners.

Using Sources 1, 2 and 3 above and opposite, **which option would you choose**?

Give reasons to **support** your choice.

Explain why you did not make the other choice.

Your answer must be based on all the Sources.

(10 marks)

NOW GO TO SECTION C ON PAGE 15

[BLANK PAGE]

SECTION C – INTERNATIONAL ISSUES

Answer **ONE** question only:

   Question 5 Study Theme 3A – The Republic of South Africa on pages 15–19
OR Question 6 Study Theme 3B – The People's Republic of China on pages 21–25
OR Question 7 Study Theme 3C – The United States of America on pages 27–31
OR Question 8 Study Theme 3D – The European Union on pages 33–37
OR Question 9 Study Theme 3E – Development in Brazil on pages 39–43

STUDY THEME 3A: THE REPUBLIC OF SOUTH AFRICA

> **In your answers you should give examples from South Africa**

Question 5

(*a*) | Housing conditions in the townships of South Africa have improved.

Describe, **in detail**, **two** ways housing conditions in the townships of South Africa have improved.

(4 marks)

(*b*) | Many people in South Africa have poor health.

Explain, **in detail**, why many people in South Africa have poor health.

(6 marks)

[Turn over

Question 5 (continued)

(c)   Study Sources 1, 2 and 3 below and opposite, then answer the question which follows.

SOURCE 1

Percentage of Votes and Seats won by the African National Congress (ANC) in the National Assembly 1999 and 2004

Year	Percentage (%) votes	Seats won
1999	66·3%	266
2004	69·6%	279

Votes cast for the ANC by Province

Province	1999	2004
Western Cape	682,748	740,077
Northern Cape	211,206	222,205
Free State	887,091	838,583
Gauteng	2,527,676	2,408,821
KwaZulu Natal	1,176,926	1,312,767
Limpopo	1,483,199	1,487,168
North West	1,052,895	1,083,254
Mpumalanga	962,260	979,155
Eastern Cape	1,617,329	1,806,221
Total South Africa	10,601,330	10,878,251

SOURCE 2

Public Opinion Poll — Voter Support for ANC, 2004

Age	Percentage (%) saying "I am an ANC supporter"	Percentage (%) saying "I am not an ANC supporter"
18–24 years	78%	21%
25–34 years	76%	23%
35–49 years	75%	24%
50+ years	62%	35%
Race		
Black	85%	14%
White	5%	92%
Coloured	43%	55%
Indian	38%	56%

Question 5 (*c*) (continued)

SOURCE 3

ANC Support in South Africa

Despite having a constitution and electoral system that encourages multi-party democracy, South Africa has been dominated by one party over the last 10 years. The 2004 election results confirmed that the African National Congress (ANC) is the most popular party across the country.

The ANC, however, does not have the support of all voters. There is a growing racial divide in support for the ANC. In an opinion poll carried out in 2004, 26·3% of all registered voters said they did not support the ANC. Of these voters, 70% said they supported another party. The Democratic Alliance is now backed by three quarters of Whites and nearly 70% of Coloured people. The Democratic Alliance won 50 of the 400 seats in the National Assembly in 2004.

For the foreseeable future, however, it would seem that the ANC will continue to dominate South African politics. The Democratic Alliance has strong support in the Western Cape and the Inkatha Freedom Party has many supporters in KwaZulu Natal. Despite this, at the 2006 local government elections the ANC gained more votes, won more seats and took control of more councils than ever before in a local government election.

Support for the ANC has increased between 1999 and 2004 and it still remains popular amongst all groups.

View of ANC member

Using Sources 1, 2 and 3 above and opposite, give **two** reasons to **support** and **two** reasons to **oppose** the view of the ANC member.

Your answer must be based entirely on the Sources.

You must use information from each Source in your answer.

(8 marks)

[Turn over

Question 5 (continued)

(d)   Study Sources 1, 2 and 3 below and opposite, then answer the question which follows.

SOURCE 1

Challenges Facing Education in South Africa

Education in South Africa has seen huge changes over the years since Apartheid ended. Pupils are no longer sent to different schools by law, because of their race. Many schools are now integrated and all pupils, not only Whites, are entitled to a high standard of education. Compared with most countries, education receives a big slice of government funding, usually at least 20% of the total budget. Some Whites are unhappy that the huge advantage they had in access to the best education, compared to other races, has now gone.

Although the Government is trying to address the inequalities in education as a result of 40 years of Apartheid rule, the legacy lingers on. The greatest challenges lie in poorer, rural provinces like Mpumalanga and the Eastern Cape. In the wealthier provinces, schools are generally better resourced.

The pass rate for the Matric exam (taken by senior pupils) is still lower for girls than boys. In 2005, 67·2% of girls passed compared to 69·7% of boys. Older women have little education compared to men. However, Matric exam pass rates are steadily improving in South Africa. Racial differences in education still remain; for example, Blacks have less education and gain fewer qualifications compared to other racial groups.

Despite the problems, there are improvements over the years. Every year many new classrooms are being built and more teachers employed. A new curriculum was introduced in 2006 for grades 10 to 12. This places more emphasis on life skills, mathematical literacy as well as African history and culture. Skills will be developed in Information Technology to prepare students for a modern world.

SOURCE 2

Province of South Africa	Percentage (%) of children aged 7-15 attending school	Percentage (%) pass rate in the Matric exam
Western Cape	98·2%	84·4%
Northern Cape	96·1%	78·9%
Free State	97·5%	77·8%
Gauteng	99·0%	74·9%
KwaZulu Natal	97·0%	70·5%
Limpopo	92·4%	64·9%
North West	97·9%	63·0%
Mpumalanga	97·8%	58·6%
Eastern Cape	97·4%	56·7%

Question 5 (*d*) (continued)

SOURCE 3

Level of Education achieved by Persons aged 20+

Race	No schooling	Up to Primary Only	Some Secondary	Completed Secondary ("Matric")	Higher Education
Black	22·3%	25·4%	30·4%	16·8%	5·2%
Coloured	8·3%	28·2%	40·1%	18·5%	4·9%
Asian	5·3%	11·9%	33·0%	34·9%	14·9%
White	1·4%	2·0%	25·9%	40·9%	29·8%

Percentage (%) of Persons (aged 20+) with no formal Education

	2002	2005
Male	9·9%	5·2%
Female	14·0%	12·2%

Using Sources 1, 2 and 3 above and opposite, what **conclusions** can be drawn about education in South Africa?

You should reach conclusions about at least **three** of the following:

* provincial differences in education

* gender differences in education

* racial differences in education

* differences in education over time.

You must use information from all the Sources. You should compare information within and between the Sources.

(8 marks)

NOW CHECK THAT YOU HAVE ANSWERED ONE QUESTION FROM EACH OF SECTIONS A, B AND C

[BLANK PAGE]

STUDY THEME 3B: THE PEOPLE'S REPUBLIC OF CHINA

> **In your answers you should give examples from China**

Question 6

(a)

> Political participation is limited in China.

Describe, **in detail**, **two** ways in which political participation is limited in China.

(4 marks)

(b)

> In China, there has been a large movement of people from the countryside to urban areas in recent years.

Explain, **in detail**, why there has been a large movement of people from the countryside to urban areas in China in recent years.

(6 marks)

[Turn over

Question 6 (continued)

(c) Study Sources 1, 2 and 3 below and opposite, then answer the question which follows.

SOURCE 1

Economic Expansion in China

China has changed a great deal in recent years and its economy has become one of the largest in the world. For some people this is good news as they have benefited from better jobs and higher wages. They are able to afford products which make life easier for them, such as household appliances. This, in turn, means that more goods are produced to meet demand and this further helps the Chinese economy.

There are also a large number of people who have lost their jobs due to new technology. Machines and computers now do the work once carried out by people. For example, in the countryside many farm workers have lost their jobs, although for those who are still involved in agriculture, wages have increased in recent years.

Many firms in China have to compete against one another and with firms in other countries. Sometimes, profit comes before health and safety and there has been an increase in the number of accidents and deaths because of dangerous machinery or unhealthy working conditions in factories.

While managers and workers in technology jobs have benefited from increased profits and wages, manual workers in factories, chemical plants and coal mines are risking their lives.

SOURCE 2

Year	Average Wages in Urban and Rural Areas (in Yuan)		Number of Unemployed Farm Workers
	Urban	Rural	Number
2000	4850	1190	5,000,000
2001	5900	1256	12,000,000
2002	6250	1656	23,000,000
2003	7137	1876	32,000,000
2004	7436	2105	41,000,000
2005	8020	2405	50,000,000

Question 6 (c) (continued)

SOURCE 3

Urban Households with Selected Appliances, 2000 and 2005

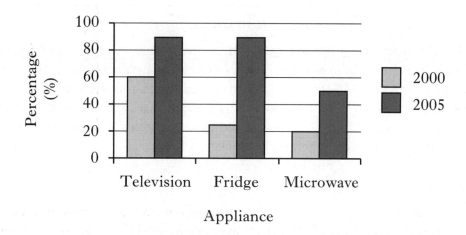

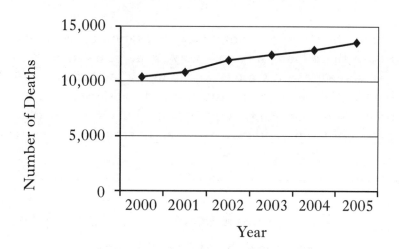

Workplace Deaths in China, 2000–2005

China's growing economy has brought many benefits.

View of Xing Zhigang

Using Sources 1, 2 and 3 above and opposite, give **two** reasons to **support** and **two** reasons to **oppose** the view of Xing Zhigang.

Your answer must be based entirely on the Sources.

You must use information from each Source in your answer.

(8 marks)

[Turn over

Question 6 (continued)

(*d*)   Study Sources 1, 2 and 3 below and opposite, then answer the question which follows.

SOURCE 1

Education in China

There are different levels of education in China. From age 6 to 12, children attend elementary (primary) school, followed by 3 years at junior high school and finally, from ages 15 to 18, senior high school. Primary and junior high schools are directly funded by local taxes. As rural areas tend to be poorer than urban areas, there is less money to spend on education. A lack of money means that schools have large classes and cannot afford the best teachers and good teaching materials. The result of poor teaching, large classes and poor resources is that pupils lose motivation, are less likely to pass exams and may not get well paid jobs in the future.

In recent years, China has made economic reforms and national government spending on education has been reduced. This affects rural areas more and the Government has been working to support education in these areas. One successful initiative is the "volunteer team of university students to support the countryside" where university students help in rural schools.

In most areas of China, the nine year compulsory education initiative has been adopted. All pupils should have the opportunity to receive nine years primary and junior high school education. In some areas of China, mostly in the far western, mainly rural parts, many pupils receive less than nine years education. In rural schools, girls tend to enrol less as they get older. Although gender equality in China is better than in many other countries, in rural areas of China, girls are expected to attend to domestic duties as they reach their teens.

SOURCE 2

Urban and Rural Comparisons

	Rural Areas	Urban Areas
Enrolment in Elementary School	96%	99%
Enrolment in Junior High School	92%	99%
Enrolment in Senior High School	20%	70%
Percentage of well-qualified teachers	42%	90%
Percentage of schools with good resources	30%	75%
Average number of pupils in a class	50	25
Spending per student in Elementary Schools	1300 yuan	1900 yuan
Spending per student in Junior High Schools	1500 yuan	2300 yuan
Spending per student in Senior High Schools	2700 yuan	3800 yuan

Question 6 (d) (continued)

SOURCE 3

School Enrolment in China by Gender and Area

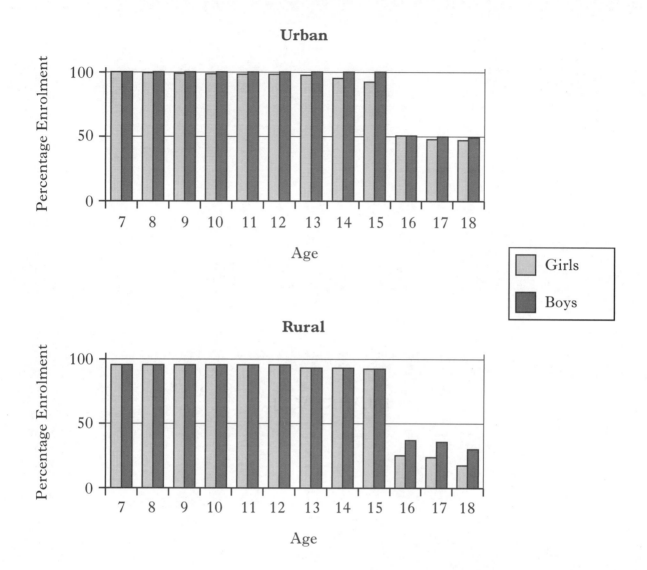

Using Sources 1, 2 and 3 above and opposite, what **conclusions** can be drawn about education in China?

You should reach conclusions about at least **three** of the following:

• differences in spending on education between urban and rural areas

• gender differences in education

• enrolment in schools in urban and rural areas

• differences in the quality of education in urban and rural areas.

You must use information from all the Sources. You should compare information within and between the Sources.

(8 marks)

NOW CHECK THAT YOU HAVE ANSWERED ONE QUESTION FROM EACH OF SECTIONS A, B AND C

[BLANK PAGE]

STUDY THEME 3C: THE UNITED STATES OF AMERICA

In your answers you should give examples from the USA

Question 7

(a)

> There are inequalities in health between different ethnic groups in the USA.

Describe, **in detail**, **two** inequalities in health between different ethnic groups in the USA.

(4 marks)

(b)

> Women and ethnic minorities are poorly represented in the US political system.

Explain, **in detail**, why women and ethnic minorities are poorly represented in the US political system.

(6 marks)

[Turn over

Question 7 (continued)

(*c*)   Study Sources 1, 2 and 3 below and opposite, then answer the question which follows.

SOURCE 1

Immigration into the USA

There are thought to be about 11·5 million illegal immigrants in the United States, and each year between half a million and a million more enter illegally into the country, mostly through the 2,000-mile (3,200-km) southern border with Mexico. Overall, illegal immigrants account for 3·6% of the total US population.

Many of these people are poorly educated, unskilled workers. In their thousands, they fill the sort of jobs that most native-born Americans will not take, at least not for the same pay. Much of California's agriculture relies on immigrant labour. Supporters of continuing immigration say that immigrants are good for the economy. Their low wages keep prices in the US low and they also pay taxes. Opponents of continuing immigration say uncontrolled immigration causes unemployment because immigrants are highly concentrated in certain industries. This puts those already in the US out of work as illegal immigrants are competing with young people, ethnic minorities and recently arrived legal immigrants for jobs.

Those who are in favour of more immigration say that the USA is a nation of immigrants and that immigrants come to America to work hard and enjoy the "American Dream" like millions before them. Those who are against more immigration say it places too great a strain on welfare services in states like California, Texas and Florida where many of them settle.

SOURCE 2
Selected Industries with a High Proportion of Illegal Immigrants

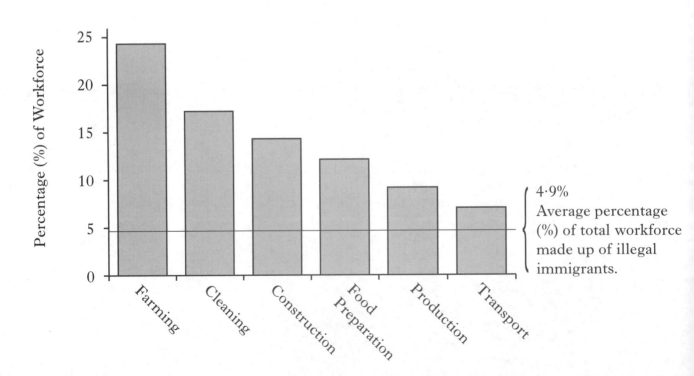

4·9%
Average percentage (%) of total workforce made up of illegal immigrants.

Question 7 (c) (continued)

SOURCE 3

Survey of Public Opinion on Attitudes towards Immigration and Immigrants: 2006

	Percentage (%) agreeing with statement
Immigrants today . . .	
• are a burden because they take jobs and housing	52%
• strengthen the US with their hard work and talents	41%
Growing numbers of newcomers from other countries . . .	
• threaten traditional American customs and values	48%
• strengthen American society	45%
Immigrants from Latin America . . .	
• work very hard	80%
• have strong family values	80%
• often go on welfare	37%
• significantly increase crime	33%

Continuing immigration benefits the USA and is supported by most Americans.

View of Alejandro Escovedo

Using Sources 1, 2 and 3 above and opposite, give **two** reasons to **support** and **two** reasons to **oppose** the view of Alejandro Escovedo.

Your answer must be based entirely on the Sources.

You must use information from each Source in your answer.

(8 marks)

[Turn over

Question 7 (continued)

(d)   Study Sources 1, 2 and 3 below and opposite, then answer the question which follows.

SOURCE 1

Education in the USA

The population of the United States is becoming better educated. Significant differences in educational attainment remain with regard to race and ethnic origin and whether someone was born in the USA or is foreign born.

In 2003, over four-fifths (84·6%) of all adults 25 years or older reported they had completed at least high school; more than half (52·5%) had spent some time taking part in or completing a college course and over one in four adults (27·2%) had attained a university degree. All measures are record levels.

Traditionally, as the most successful ethnic group in the USA, White Americans have had educational advantages. They usually live in areas with good schools, even being able to afford private education and go on to higher education. Asian Americans seem to believe strongly in the importance of education in achieving the American Dream, with many Asians achieving great success in education. While many Black Americans are making progress in education, some are disadvantaged by social and economic inequalities. Language barriers can be a problem for some Hispanic Americans, especially those who have arrived recently or whose parents only speak Spanish at home.

SOURCE 2

Percentage (%) achieving Level of Educational Attainment, by Race or Ethnic Group

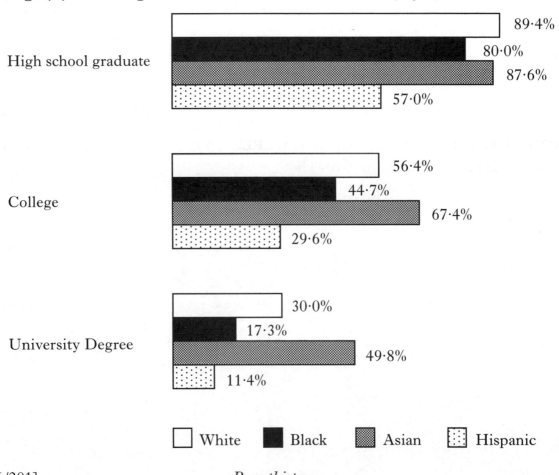

Question 7 (*d*) (continued)

SOURCE 3

Educational Attainment of foreign born Americans

	Percentage (%) achieving High School Graduation level	Percentage (%) achieving College level	Percentage (%) achieving University Degree
White	86·1%	56·8%	37·6%
Black	77·3%	47·6%	25·4%
Asian	86·6%	66·1%	50·1%
Hispanic	44·7%	21·5%	9·8%

Using Sources 1, 2 and 3 above and opposite, what **conclusions** can be drawn about education in the USA?

You should reach conclusions about at least **three** of the following:

- White Americans compared to other racial and ethnic groups

- Black Americans compared to other racial and ethnic groups

- Asian Americans compared to other racial and ethnic groups

- Hispanic Americans compared to other racial and ethnic groups.

You must use information from all the Sources. You should compare information within and between the Sources.

(8 marks)

NOW CHECK THAT YOU HAVE ANSWERED ONE QUESTION FROM EACH OF SECTIONS A, B AND C

[BLANK PAGE]

STUDY THEME 3D: THE EUROPEAN UNION

In your answers you should give examples from European Union member states

Question 8

(*a*) | European Union member states benefit from military cooperation.

Describe, **in detail**, **two** ways European Union member states benefit from military cooperation.

(4 marks)

(*b*) | People who live in the European Union can benefit from the Single European Market.

Explain, **in detail**, why people who live in the European Union can benefit from the Single European Market.

(6 marks)

[Turn over

Question 8 (continued)

(c)   Study Sources 1, 2 and 3 below and opposite, then answer the question which follows.

SOURCE 1

Migration of Workers in European Union Member States

Since the enlargement of the European Union in 2004, many people from the new member states have taken up residence in other countries. Better employment prospects and a better standard of living have attracted them to countries such as France and the United Kingdom. Some people argue that the UK has been allowing too many immigrants in from countries such as Poland and Hungary and that this will lead to unemployment for British citizens.

Others argue that the new immigrants are good for Britain and they are taking up jobs which are vacant and which British people do not want. Furthermore, the British-born population is declining and Britain and other European countries need an influx of workers to help the economy. Many employers are happy with the standard of work carried out by new immigrants and comment on their positive attitudes, such as punctuality, hard work and a willingness to learn about the job.

Since enlargement, it has been estimated that over 400,000 people came to Britain in one year to make a living, a higher figure than expected. Recently, concern has been raised that many more Eastern Europeans will come here to work. If unemployment increases, new immigrants will claim benefits and this will be a drain on the British economy and taxes will be increased for all workers. Others argue that British-born people leave the country to seek work in other states, and everyone should be free to go and live where they like.

SOURCE 2

Migration in and out of the UK, 2000–2005   **Number of Births in the UK in Millions**

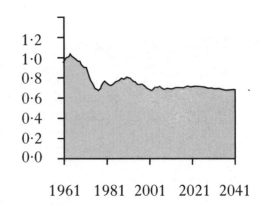

- ◆ Immigration into the UK
- ■ Emigration out of the UK

Question 8 (c) (continued)

SOURCE 3

Shortages in the UK workforce		UK Benefits claimed by Eastern European Immigrants (2005)		
Selected Industries	Shortage (%)	Type of Benefit	Number of people paid	Average Amount per person
Skilled Trades	39%	Income Support	193	£57·45
Customer Services	20%	Jobseeker's Allowance	564	£57·45
General Office Positions	17%	Pension Credit	11	£114·05
Road Haulage Drivers	25%	Child Benefit	22,280	£17·45
Health Care Workers	27%	Family Tax Credit	14,009	£5,200·00
		Housing Benefit	110	£100·00
		Homeless Payments	453	£100·00

> Immigration, into the UK, of people from the new member states of the EU brings many advantages.

View of Keith Angus

Using Sources 1, 2 and 3 above and opposite, give **two** reasons to **support** and **two** reasons to **oppose** the view of Keith Angus.

Your answer must be based entirely on the Sources.

You must use information from each Source in your answer.

(8 marks)

[Turn over

Question 8 (continued)

(d)   Study Sources 1, 2 and 3 below and opposite, then answer the question which follows.

SOURCE 1

Comparison of Schools in Germany, France, Italy and the UK

In Germany, children attend Kindergarten (nursery) until the age of 6 and primary school from age 6 to 10. At 10, depending on their grades, they may go on to a basic school until 9th grade, middle school until 10th grade or higher school, known as the Gymnasium, until 13th grade. Only this last group can go on to university.

French children also attend nursery until the age of 6 followed by primary school until the age of 11. They then go on to lower secondary, known as collège, from age 11 to 15; followed by a choice of attending either the more vocational technical college or the more academic lycée.

In Italy, young people can attend nursery as young as age 3. They go to primary school at age 6, followed by middle school at age 11 and, finally, secondary school for 5 years from age 14 to 19, although some leave after age 16.

In the UK, young people attend nursery school for a year or two until the age of 4 or 5, primary school until age 11 or 12, and secondary school until they are at least 16.

Spending on education at each level varies from country to country. For example, some countries spend more on the secondary sector than on nursery education. There is also a variation in spending per pupil in each country and this might have an effect on the number of pupils per teacher. The maximum number of pupils per classroom is not the same in each country nor in different levels of primary school.

SOURCE 2

Pupil Teacher Ratios and Maximum Class Sizes

Country	Maximum Number of Pupils per Classroom		Ratio of Pupils to Teachers at Secondary School
	Primary 1–3	Primary 4–7	
Germany	30	30	15:1
France	30	30	12:1
Italy	25	25	11:1
UK	30	33	15:1

Question 8 (*d*) (continued)

SOURCE 3

Percentage (%) Spent on Level of Education

Country	Nursery	Primary	Secondary	Post Secondary
Germany	22%	24%	30%	24%
France	24%	24%	27%	25%
UK	26%	23%	28%	23%
Italy	21%	29%	28%	22%

Spending per Pupil at Secondary and Primary Levels

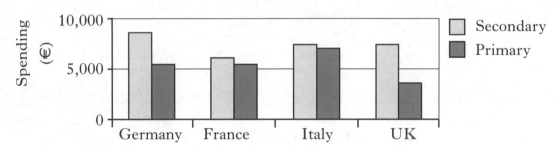

Using Sources 1, 2 and 3 above and opposite, what **conclusions** can be drawn about education in different EU countries?

You should reach conclusions about at least **three** of the following:

- education in Germany compared with other countries

- education in France compared with other countries

- education in Italy compared with other countries

- education in the UK compared with other countries.

You must use information from all the Sources. You should compare information within and between the Sources.

(8 marks)

NOW CHECK THAT YOU HAVE ANSWERED ONE QUESTION FROM EACH OF SECTIONS A, B AND C

[BLANK PAGE]

STUDY THEME 3E: DEVELOPMENT IN BRAZIL

> **In your answers you should give examples from Brazil**

Question 9

(a)
> The living conditions of people in the favelas of Brazil have improved in recent years.

Describe, **in detail**, **two** ways in which the living conditions of people in the favelas of Brazil have improved in recent years.

(4 marks)

(b)
> Land ownership continues to be a problem in Brazil.

Explain, **in detail**, why land ownership continues to be a problem in Brazil.

(6 marks)

[Turn over

Question 9 (continued)

(*c*) Study Sources 1, 2 and 3 below and opposite, then answer the question which follows.

SOURCE 1

2006 Brazil Presidential Election Results

	1st round		2nd round	
Candidates	**Votes**	**%**	**Votes**	**%**
Luiz Inácio (Lula) da Silva	46,662,365	48·61	58,295,042	60·83
Geraldo Alckmin	39,968,369	41·64	37,543,178	39·17
Heloísa Helena	6,575,393	6·85	-	-
Cristovam Buarque	2,538,844	2·64	-	-
Ana Maria Rangel	126,404	0·13	-	-
José Maria Eymael	63,294	0·07	-	-
Luciano Bivar	62,064	0·06	-	-
Total (turnout 83·2%)	**95,996,733**	**100·00**	**95,838,220**	**100.00**

SOURCE 2

% Votes gained by the two main Presidential Candidates

Regional Votes — 2nd Round

Regions of Brazil	Luiz Inácio (Lula) da Silva	Geraldo Alckmin
North	65·6%	34·4%
Northeast	77·1%	22·9%
Middle-West	52·4%	47·6%
Southeast	56·9%	43·1%
South	46·5%	53·5%

Question 9 (*c*) (continued)

SOURCE 3

Lula elected President for a second Term

Brazilian President Luiz Inácio da Silva, popularly known as Lula, was re-elected in the country's second round of Presidential elections. It had been predicted that Lula would have gained the 50% of the votes required in the first round to win. Lula, however, faced strong opposition in the first round election and the results indicated that he did not have the support of everyone in Brazil.

His party had lost support after allegations of corruption involving six senior members. Although President Lula moved quickly to contain the damage by sacking his campaign manager, his popularity declined in the opinion polls. Lula has also lost the support of some voters due to his economic policy which resulted in challenges to his re-election from some former supporters.

Lula's main rival, Geraldo Alckmin viewed the first round results as a triumph. He gained strong support in some regions of Brazil. In the first round election, he won 11 of the country's 27 states including his home state of Sao Paulo, Brazil's most populous state. Mr Alckmin remains popular with wealthy, middle class Brazilians and the business community.

The second round election result, however, shows that Lula still has strong support among many Brazilians. Most of the poor people in Brazil voted for Lula. He won huge victories in poor north eastern states and also took Minas Gerais and Rio de Janeiro, the country's second and third most populated states.

The Presidential election result showed that Lula is popular across all of Brazil.

View of Ferreira Martins

Using Sources 1, 2 and 3 above and opposite, give **two** reasons to **support** and **two** reasons to **oppose** the view of Ferreira Martins.

Your answer must be based entirely on the Sources.

You must use information from each Source in your answer.

(8 marks)

[Turn over

Question 9 (continued)

(*d*)　Study Sources 1, 2 and 3 below and opposite, then answer the question which follows.

SOURCE 1

Education in Brazil

The Constitution guarantees the right of all Brazilian citizens to eight years of education. Despite education being guaranteed to all citizens, there are sixteen million Brazilians aged over 15 years who are unable to read and write. Although literacy is improving, different levels still exist between the regions. In the Northeast, 24·3% cannot read and write. This is twice the national average and more than three times the rate in the South. Although there has been an increase in the enrolment and attendance of young people in school, regional differences remain.

There are also racial differences in education. Almost 8% of young adult white and Asian people are illiterate, compared to 16·6% of black and mixed race people. Gender differences in education are improving as more girls are enrolled and attend school than in the past, especially in secondary education.

The Ministry of Education has tried to address the problems in education by giving financial support to develop programmes aimed at providing education to those young people and adults who are illiterate. In 2003, over R189 (Real) million was given to the North and Northeast where there is more poverty; this increased to R340 million in 2004. There is also a government incentive programme called "Bolsa Familia" that gives parents about R7 per month for sending their children to school.

SOURCE 2

Enrolment in Primary and Secondary School by Gender (2004)

Enrolment	Primary School	Secondary School
Female	91%	78%
Male	98%	72%

Attendance Rate by Level of Education and Race (2004)

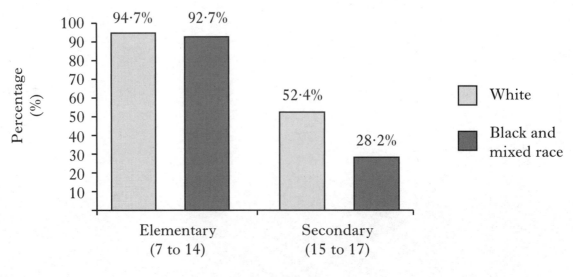

Question 9 (d) (continued)

SOURCE 3

Percentage (%) Attendance in Primary and Secondary Education by Region

Region	Secondary Schools		Primary Schools	
	1992	2002	1992	2002
North	76·8%	87·5%	82·5%	92·1%
Northeast	61·7%	86·6%	69·7%	91·6%
Southeast	86·9%	92·6%	88·0%	95·2%
South	88·3%	91·9%	86·9%	95·8%
Centre-West	84·0%	89·2%	85·9%	93·8%

Using Sources 1, 2 and 3 above and opposite, what **conclusions** can be drawn about education in Brazil?

You should reach conclusions about at least **three** of the following:

- gender differences in education
- racial differences in education
- regional differences in education
- improvements in education.

You must use information from all the Sources. You should compare information within and between the Sources.

(8 marks)

NOW CHECK THAT YOU HAVE ANSWERED ONE QUESTION FROM EACH OF SECTIONS A, B AND C

[END OF QUESTION PAPER]

Acknowledgements

Leckie & Leckie is grateful to the copyright holders, as credited, for permission to use their material:
The Economist for the article 'China and Drugs- The Kindness Treatment' © The Economist Newspaper Limited, London 02/12/99 (2006 p 33); and the article 'China's Health Care' © The Economist Newspaper Limited, London 21/08/04 (2006 p 35).

The following companies/individuals have very generously given permission to reproduce their copyright material free of charge:
Her Majesty's Stationary Office for a chart © Crown copyright (2005 p 20);
The Electoral Commission for two tables (2005 p 8);
YouGov for a chart taken from a survey 2003 (2006 p9);
The Office for National Statistics for a table from 'Patterns of Pay: Results of 2002
New Earnings Survey Table 1 P644' by Joanna Bulman (2006 p 12); and a text adapted from 'Labour Market Trends 2002' (2006 p 13); and a diagram from' Smoking Statistics' (2006 p 16);
Her Majesty's Stationary Office for a table from Scottish Social Statistics © Crown copyright (2006 p 20); and a table from Social Trends © Crown copyright (2006 p 24);
South Africa Police Service for the text 'Crime in South Africa' (2006 p 37).